ACROSS OKA

Across Oka was premièred by the Royal ⬛⬛⬛⬛⬛⬛⬛⬛⬛⬛⬛⬛⬛⬛e, Stratford-upon-Avon, in April 1988.

'Robert Holman's *Across Oka* is about me⬛⬛⬛⬛⬛⬛⬛⬛⬛⬛⬛⬛⬛⬛⬛⬛s of passionate, gentle people in north York⬛⬛⬛⬛⬛⬛⬛⬛⬛⬛⬛⬛⬛o all experience, the second constrained by t⬛⬛⬛⬛⬛⬛⬛ state . . . the new play is alive with theatrical confrontation and generosity of spirit.'

Michael Ratcliffe, *Observer*

Robert Holman, author of *Today* and *Making Noise Quietly*, 'continues gently and unpretentiously to build himself a formidable reputation.'

Benedict Nightingale, *New Statesman*

ROBERT HOLMAN was born in 1952 in Guisborough, Cleveland. He received an Arts Council Writer's Bursary in 1974 and his plays include *Mud* (Royal Court Sunday Night production, 1974); *The Natural Cause* (Cockpit Theatre, 1974); *Outside the Whale* (Traverse Theatre, Edinburgh, 1976); *German Skerries* (Bush Theatre, London, 1977), for which he received the George Devine Award; *Rooting* (Traverse Theatre, Edinburgh, 1979); *The Estuary* (Bush Theatre, London, 1980); *Other Worlds* (Royal Court, 1983); *Today* (Royal Shakespeare Company, 1984); *The Overgrown Path* (Royal Court, 1985); *Making Noise Quietly* (Bush Theatre, London, 1987); *Across Oka* (Royal Shakespeare Company, 1988) and *Rafts and Dreams* (Royal Court Theatre, 1990). Robert Holman's television plays include *Chance of a Lifetime* (BBC, 1980) and *This is History, Gran* (BBC, 1986).

The front cover shows children clearing up for May Day in Bratsk, Siberia. Photograph © Robert Holman.

ACROSS OKA

ROBERT HOLMAN

Methuen Drama

A METHUEN NEW THEATRESCRIPT

First published in Great Britain as a paperback original by
Methuen Drama, Michelin House, 81 Fulham Road, London SW3 6RB
and distributed in the United States of America by HEB Inc,
361 Hanover Street, New Hampshire NH 03801 3959

Printed in England by Clays Ltd, St Ives plc

British Library Cataloguing in Publication Data

Holman, Robert, *1952 –*
 Across Oka. – (A Methuen new theatrescript)
 I. Title
 822'.914

 ISBN 0-413-19360-8

To
Ann and Mark
Emma and Paul
Robin, Tammy and Sam

Across Oka was first performed by the Royal Shakespeare Company at the Other Place, Stratford-upon-Avon on 13 April 1988. The cast was as follows:

JOLYON	Alfred Burke
MATTY	Edward Rawle-Hicks
EILEEN	Patricia Lawrence
TESSA	Jane Cox
PAVEL	Richard Haddon Haines
MARGARET	Joan Blackham
NIKOLAI	Timothy Stark

Musicians: Jennifer Nole (Violin), Kate Stott (Piano)

Directed by Sarah Pia Anderson
Designed by Ashley Martin-Davis
Lighting by Geraint Pughe
Music by Ilona Sekacz
Stage Manager Maggie Mackay
Deputy Stage Manager Martyn Sergent
Assistant Stage Manager Steve Lillywhite

The play is set in the summer of 1986 and the spring of 1987.

ACT ONE

Scene One

The cobbled backyard of a small terraced house. A warm July afternoon.

The four sides of the yard incline slightly towards the centre where there is a drain covered by a metal grid. Two wooden kitchen chairs are set apart from one another. On one of them is a lace-making board with some lace in progress, and on the ground is a newspaper which is open at the crossword, a dictionary, and a biro.

JOLYON is sitting in the other chair. There is his cardigan draped over the back, and on the ground is a library book. On his lap is a wooden box in a plastic Boots carrier bag.

JOLYON is a tall, thin, dignified man of seventy-four, with a shock of white hair. He is wearing socks, sandals, trousers, and a shirt with the sleeves rolled to the elbow.

MATTY is standing beside him.

MATTY is a young, fresh-faced, fair-haired boy of sixteen. He is cleanly dressed in good trainers, jeans, and a t-shirt. He is wearing an expensive wristwatch.

JOLYON: Aram Kabalevsky was my best friend. We were both eight. His parents were refugees from Tsarist old Russia, although he was born here. I remember saying to Aram: how can you return when you've never been there? He said: my dad knows Vladimir Ilyich Lenin, and we're going.

A slight pause.

A year later I was in bed, Matty, when my mother called up the stairs. I can still hear her voice. I came down in my brother's pyjamas and there was a gentleman on the doorstep. My mother said: this gentleman's Russian, Jolly. He said: was I Jolyon Davis, he had a present from my best friend who'd returned to the Soviet Union.

He takes the box from the carrier bag. It is roughly made and was nailed together many years ago by a child.

It was this. With it was a letter from Aram which I must've lost. I tried writing back to the address, but nothing ever happened. I think eventually the post office decided it was impossible to write to Russia. My friend had disappeared again.

EILEEN enters from the house. She is carrying a small plate on which is a slice of fruit-cake.

EILEEN is a thin woman of seventy. Her hair is neatly done. She is wearing a short-sleeved cotton dress, stockings, and stoutish shoes.

EILEEN takes the plate to MATTY.

EILEEN: It's lovely to see you.

JOLYON: Of course it is.

EILEEN: Don't wait to be asked.

MATTY smiles, he begins to eat the cake.

EILEEN goes to her chair and sits down. She picks up the lace-making board, but she doesn't work at it.

JOLYON: A month ago we were watching a wildlife programme on the television. It was mostly about the Siberian Crane, which is now almost extinct in Russia. It's been pillaged and its habitats have been destroyed. In America – where was it?

EILEEN: A place called the International Crane Foundation, in Wisconsin.

JOLYON: In Wisconsin they're now breeding these Siberian Cranes. They've taken some eggs from the very north of Siberia, hatched them in America, and now they're hoping to take some eggs from those birds back to Russia, and put them back into the wild.

MATTY: I think I saw it.

EILEEN: Have you got a television at school?

MATTY: We have occasionally.

JOLYON: It wouldn't mean anything t'you, but the Russian ornithologist in the programme was called Professor Pavel Kabalevsky. Can you guess what Aram Kabalevsky's present was all those years ago?

EILEEN: Don't tease him.

MATTY: What?

JOLYON: Have a guess.

He taps the box.

What's in here?

EILEEN: Jolyon.

MATTY: I don't know, it could be anything.

JOLYON: It couldn't you know.

EILEEN: Don't encourage 'im, Matty.

MATTY: A bomb. Or something.

EILEEN: He wants you to make a fool of yourself.

JOLYON: I don't.

JOLYON taps the box.

MATTY: You're succeeding, Grandpa.

JOLYON: Think about what I've told you.

A slight pause.

EILEEN: Jolly, do stop it, it isn't fair. Let him eat his cake in peace.

JOLYON lifts the lid from the box.

MATTY: Eggs.

JOLYON: Not just any eggs.

MATTY: What? Siberian Crane eggs? Really?

JOLYON: Yes.

MATTY: Wow.

The two eggs are nestled in two recesses within the box.

MATTY kneels to look more closely.

Where did he get them from?

JOLYON: Siberia, I suppose. We collected eggs. Many boys did.

MATTY: Why haven't I seen them before?

JOLYON: They've been tucked away in the loft.

MATTY: I hate to say it, Jolly, but this is probably why they're extinct.

JOLYON: I know.

MATTY: Your friend didn't seem to care terribly much.

EILEEN: I think you can be too hard on a small child, Matty. Especially then.

MATTY *finishes his cake.*

MATTY: What are you going to do with them?

JOLYON: Nothing.

MATTY *takes an egg from the box.*

MATTY: May I have one of them?

JOLYON: No. Not yet.

MATTY *holds the egg up to the sun.*

I wondered if there was a connection. What do you think?

MATTY: I don't know.

EILEEN: If you tell him there is, you'll make his year.

JOLYON: It's the two names. Kabalevsky.

EILEEN: Jolly. Honestly.

JOLYON: I think it's possible. What d'you think?

MATTY: Why don't you write to the BBC? Or something.

EILEEN: He has already. He sits by the letterbox every morning as if it was his birthday.

JOLYON: I'd like us t'go t'Russia, Matty. But yer Gran won't. I know one of us has to be a little bit sensible – but we're in our dotage, why ever not?

EILEEN: Jolyon.

JOLYON: She hates anyone with a dream.

MATTY *puts the egg back in the box.*

MATTY: Thank you for the cake.

EILEEN: You're welcome.

JOLYON: She does. Always has.

EILEEN: Would you like another piece?

MATTY: I've had sufficient thanks.

EILEEN: You're an old bugger, Jolyon. Stop it.

JOLYON (*quietly*): I'm an old bugger.

EILEEN: Stop asking Matty to take sides, it isn't fair.

JOLYON: What d'you think? You'd go, wouldn't you?

A slight pause.

MATTY: I'd go, Gran. I think I would.

JOLYON: There you are, love.

MATTY: I didn't mean I'd definitely go.

EILEEN: Since that television programme, Matty, we've had nothing but this.

JOLYON: What's wrong with it?

EILEEN: If you think we can up and gallivant across the world without a thought, you've got another think coming.

MATTY *looks down.*

Is that clear?

JOLYON: No.

MATTY *takes an egg from the box.*

EILEEN: He doesn't say how we can possibly afford an expensive holiday like that. We can't, and that's all there is to it. I wish we could.

JOLYON: At least let's dream about it.

MATTY *plays with the egg in his fingers.*

Can't we dream? Have another look at the brochure?

EILEEN: I'm heartily sick of being made the scapegoat.

EILEEN *looks down.*

JOLYON: Don't get yourself upset, love.

EILEEN: I am now.

EILEEN *looks up.*

What was that fruit-cake like?

MATTY: It was delicious.

EILEEN: When I looked I'd only half a packet of raisins.

A slight pause.

JOLYON: I wanted to show Matty the eggs. We haven't seen him for a while. We miss you when you're at school.

MATTY *smiles nervously.*

JOLYON *puts the box on the ground, he stands up, and goes to* EILEEN.

Come on, don't be silly.

EILEEN: I don't want you, Jolly.

JOLYON *kneels.*

JOLYON: Come on, no one means anything by it, least of all me.

He takes the lace-making board and puts it on the ground.

Matty can have the eggs an' then it's a finish, isn't it? I'm only joking.

EILEEN *stands up, she picks up Matty's plate, and then goes into the house.*

A pause.

JOLYON *stands up.*

I'm for the rolling-pin treatment later.

MATTY *looks up.*

She's all right, don't you worry.

MATTY: Is she?

JOLYON: Yes.

A slight pause.

MATTY: Did Gran know Aram?

JOLYON: No, she didn't. Yer gran lived in Grange Road, which was about a mile an' a half away.

He smiles.

All that part of town is unrecognizable now. Our first home together was in Bolckow Street, near the old Albert Park. It had seventeen poplars, which were notorious for shenanigins. Your mother was born at Bolckow Street. That was razed too, eventually.

MATTY *pulls the box towards himself.*

MATTY: May I have the eggs? You did just say?

JOLYON: Yes.

MATTY: I'd like to do some still-life water-colours this summer. Mum's bought me an easel.

JOLYON: Is this a new idea?

MATTY: Well, not really. I've always been fairly good. Well, it's quite new.

JOLYON: Have you any you could show us?

MATTY: I never thought. I have some – but you mustn't laugh.

JOLYON: Why?

MATTY: Well, it's so embarassing – because I did some portraits of myself. Mum found them. Only I did them when I had nothing on.

A slight pause.

JOLYON: That's all right. What's wrong with that?

MATTY: Well, at least it was year ago. If I was excellent it probably wouldn't matter. Vanity's fine when you're talented. I don't mean they're bad or anything. Juvenile, I think. You know, doing that. (*He has gone bright pink.*) Actually, Mum thought they were rather good.

JOLYON (*smiling*): They must be then. How is your Mum?

MATTY: She's still laughing at me.

JOLYON: Why don't you laugh back?

MATTY (*smiling*): Well, I've tried.

JOLYON: What happens?

MATTY: She laughs even more.

JOLYON: I wish Eileen would laugh a little bit.

He sits on his chair.

I'm having trouble with my peeing, Matty. That's what that is all about. It's getting me down, but Eileen is beside herself with worry. I said to her: we need a plumber, love. My joke about going to Russia has nothing t'do with it.

MATTY: Mum told me.

JOLYON: Yer gran is frightened, very understandably, I think. Embarrassed. Normally embarrassment is the other way about. For the first time in many years it's as if she seems to blame me. To be honest with you, I'm a little bit bitter about it. Very bitter. With her I mean. It started a few months ago with little splashes in my pants.

MATTY: Yes.

JOLYON: It's me who has to leave the room. I'm the baby. I'm the one who dribbles. I think we could afford a foreign holiday if we sold the boat. I know she isn't worth very much.

MATTY: No.

JOLYON: I wanted to ask you –

MATTY: What?

JOLYON: If you'd help me paint her and varnish her in these next few weeks?

MATTY: Yes.

JOLYON: It needn't take us more than a few days. We'd have her spanking new in no time.

MATTY: I've been sailing at school.

JOLYON: Have you? Whereabouts?

MATTY? Well, only on the river, tacking up and down.

JOLYON: What in?

MATTY: An Enterprise.

JOLYON: They're not dissimilar. Did you enjoy it?

MATTY: I enjoyed it, quite.

JOLYON: You're not a sailor, are you?

MATTY: I escaped rugger.

JOLYON: Don't you like it?

MATTY: Rugger? I bloody hate it.

JOLYON: I meant the school, you nit.

MATTY: Oh, I like the school. It positively drips with well-being. I think my probelm with Mum is that I'm cocooned a little. She from me, I mean.

JOLYON: Why's that?

MATTY: I'm not unique. We have discussed it a fair bit. Most boys feel their families don't really listen to them. Or know them. I wish Mum wasn't so liberal sometimes.

JOLYON: Are you wanting to be told off?

MATTY: I'm not saying that. Actually, I wouldn't mind occasionally.

JOLYON smiles.

JOLYON: D'you think yer Gran an' me don't listen to you?

A slight pause.

MATTY: No.

JOLYON: What a liar.

MATTY: Liar?

JOLYON: Yes. Liar.

A slight pause.

MATTY: You leave me no option but to say 'yes' then.

JOLYON: True?

MATTY: It might not be true. I don't know, Grandpa.

EILEEN *enters from the house. She is carrying a small plate with a piece of fruit-cake on it.*

EILEEN: Guess who's here?

TESSA *enters. She is carrying two more, similar kitchen chairs.*

TESSA *is a tall, thin, obviously well-heeled woman of forty-six. She is wearing a summer skirt, a blouse, and expensive sandals.*

JOLYON *stands up.*

JOLYON: We were just talking about you, love. Here, let me have those.

He takes the chairs from her.

EILEEN: I've told her what a lovely surprise it is.

MATTY *stands up.*

JOLYON: One for you, Matty.

MATTY *takes a chair from him.* JOLYON *puts the other chair down.*

TESSA *sees the eggs in the box and bends over to look at them.*

TESSA: Are these the Siberian eggs, Dad? They're much smaller than I imagined. Much more nondescript.

TESSA *picks up an egg.*

MATTY: He's given them to me.

TESSA: Have you heard from the BBC at all?

MATTY: Careful.

JOLYON: We haven't, not yet.

TESSA: Perhaps they'll still have sent it on to Moscow?

EILEEN: He shouldn't build 'is hopes up.

TESSA: It's not so far these days. I would've thought a letter had a chance.

EILEEN: He gets disappointed.

JOLYON: Nowhere in the world is very far. I keep telling 'er that.

EILEEN: It's not very far on the television. It's a long way if you have to travel.

TESSA: I don't think he's about to gallop off. Or are you?

EILEEN: I think we should trot somewhere nearer.

JOLYON: We're going to see. We would like a holiday abroad. At some point.

MATTY: I thought I'd do some water-colours. Find a setting for them.

TESSA: Are you sure, Jolly?

JOLYON: Yes.

EILEEN: Don't let him have them if you're not sure.

JOLYON: I was going to give them to him.

TESSA *puts the egg back in the box.*

EILEEN *gives* TESSA *the plate.* TESSA *holds it.*

TESSA: Have the eggs aged at all?

JOLYON: I can't really remember, you know. I was half surprised when there they were.

EILEEN: It only took him a few minutes. In the loft. I remember thinking he'd be up there all day.

JOLYON: Eileen kept calling up: had I found them?

EILEEN: You ought to look, there might be some things you would like.

TESSA: I can't think what.

EILEEN: Aren't there some photographs?

JOLYON: Yes. Of both you, and Stephen.

EILEEN: You might be interested, love.

MATTY: Yes.

JOLYON: Stephen wore your dresses, you know. I'd forgotten.

EILEEN: Lads won't even wear hand-me-downs these days.

TESSA: Who can blame them?

EILEEN: Certainly not me. I don't wish what we went through on anybody.

MATTY: He wore Mum's dresses?

EILEEN: Only when he was a toddler, an' only about the house.

TESSA: The street didn't know.

EILEEN: The street did know. Everyone did the same if you had opposite sexes. Yer just didn't let them out. One or two liked it so much, they kept it up.

JOLYON: Don't exaggerate.

EILEEN: They did. I know of one who jumped off the transporter bridge. That was the sort of world we lived in.

MATTY: Was he a transvestite?

EILEEN: I've always had a nose for the oddities.

JOLYON: You didn't tell me?

EILEEN: You never asked, you didn't need t'know. He'd just got used to dresses, being a boy amongst all those older girls.

MATTY: Was he really a transvestite?

EILEEN: I was the shoulder in Bolckow Street, Matty. It was a long time ago.

A slight pause.

JOLYON: Sit down. Come on.

JOLYON *sits in his chair,* EILEEN *in hers.* EILEEN *picks up her lace-making board.*

TESSA *begins to eat her cake.*

TESSA: What're you making?

EILEEN: It's some lace for a paperweight.

TESSA *and* MATTY *sit in their chairs.*

We've sold quite a few, haven't we?

JOLYON: Yes. Eileen an' me got married in Bolckow Street.

A slight pause.

Yer know Eileen an' me got married because we had to. An' then the baby was stillborn. It was a lovely looking thing yer gran said. They tried not to let 'er see it, but yer know what yer gran's like. Especially then.

TESSA: Dad. Honestly.

JOLYON: There was another stillborn after the first. Two girls they would have been. Eileen said to me: they can't have grown dead. To this day we don't know why. I've often wondered. I like patterns, you know. I always look for the pattern in a thing.

He leans forward

When your mum was pregnant with you, Tessa, she said: this time we don't get Mrs Colling, we get a different midwife. But in the event, you were early, so we had to. She was just round the corner in Newport Road. As I fetched 'er back I could see 'er sweating. We came in an' yer mam wouldn't have anything t'do with 'er. I said: I can't do it, Eileen. She said: you'll bloody well have to. Mrs Colling was in the kitchen, she called up the stairs: I'm going. It was pandemonium. And then yer mother called down: you'll have to do me after all, this bloody bugger is next to useless. And so she did, an' it was you. I think we knew all along it wasn't Mrs Colling, but you always look for a pattern, don't you?

TESSA: Dad.

JOLYON *sits back.*

JOLYON: In those days, Matty, men weren't involved. We kept out of it. I'd have liked to have seen a baby born. We saw one on the television, didn't we, Eileen? It was fascinating.

He leans forward.

D'you remember the damp in Bolckow Street?

TESSA: Yes, I do.

JOLYON: Yer mum used to say it was like living in the middle of a waterfall.

He sits back.

We moved here when yer mum was four and Stephen was two. It was a step up for us then. The neighbours were really stand-offish and snooty, thinking yer gran was common. She cleaned this house from top to bottom with yer mum and Stephen hanging on to her pinny.

He leans forward.

You were like a limpet, Tess. It took her three days. When she'd finished she went out into the road, stood in the middle of it, and bellowed, 'my house is cleaner than yours – there's a ten shilling note for anyone who can find even a speck of dirt in my house or on my children.' You were washed and scrubbed for the occasion, so she knew she was right. No one did come out, but yer mam had made her point.

EILEEN *looks up from her lace-making, she has tears in her eyes.*

Scene Two

The backyard. A hot early August afternoon.

Three of the kitchen chairs are set apart from one another.

MATTY, *weaing a sweatshirt, is standing by himself.*

TESSA *enters.*

TESSA: Jolly's just died.

A pause.

MATTY: I'm sorry, Mum.

A pause.

EILEEN *enters.*

EILEEN: I've put two 10p's on 'is eyes, these new pennies aren't weighty enough. It was lucky I had them in my purse.

A slight pause.

I'll wash 'im, lay 'im out. I don't want the undertaker thinking anything of us.

TESSA: I'll help you.

MATTY: I'm sorry, Gran.

EILEEN: It seems funny 'im dying during the day. You expect them to die at night, don't you? Jolly never did the obvious. This baking weather got 'im down.

A slight pause.

He stole from my purse once, you know. Stole my money. You were seven, Tessa.

It was three years after we'd moved here. He took five shillings from my purse an'
went to Scarborough. Except I didn't know it was Scarborough when he went. He
left a note on the draining-board which said: 'I've gone to find work – I'll send
back what I can – Look after the bairns – Jolly.' It was our last five shillings. I'd
earned that money skivvying up at Linthorpe Grange. When he got back, I said:
how did you get on? He said: I looked at the sea. I said: is that all yer daft
bugger? He said: yes. I said: what did you spend the five shillings on? He said: the
bus fares. I said: there's men down this street walk fifteen miles to scrat f'bits of
coal no larger than yer fingernail. He said: those same men beat the hell out their
bairns. I said: you touch my bairns and that's it. He said: that's why I went to
Scarborough. I said: it's cost me five shillings 'f'you not t'beat the bairns? He said:
yes. Then there was a loud clout from next-door as Mr Troop battered their Keith.
I thought: mebbe it is five shillings well spent. I said: how often are you going to
need five shillings? He said: never again.

She sits down.

I came down that night and he was sitting huddled in the chair with a blanket over
him. I thought: yer not so bad as to go forgetting to put my coal on my fire,
because there it was burning in the grate. I said: Jolly, if you'd been able to control
yourself, or put a sleeve on your doodah, we might never had wed. He said: yes. I
said: we can't go on hating each other. He said: no. I said: if you ever want five
shillings again you must ask.

A slight pause.

MATTY: Did he?

EILEEN: Only once, when Stephen was knocked over by that brick lorry. Stephen
    was the apple in his eye. He thought it wasn't fair, but then so much isn't, is it? He
    came and he said: I need to go, Eileen. I said: is there no more I can do, love? He
    said: no, you've done your best.

MATTY: Where did he go?

EILEEN: Scarborough.

MATTY: To look at the sea again?

EILEEN: Yes. When he got back, he said: I don't want Stephen's name mentioned in
    this house again. After five years, I thought: this is bloody daft. I said: Stephen
    would want us to remember him. Yer grandad said: yes, I was wrong. And that
    was it.

A slight pause.

MATTY: Is that why he bought the sailing dinghy?

EILEEN: He bought the boat to be on the sea. He could go anywhere in that boat.
    In his head, Matty, in his dreams.

    TESSA *picks up a chair, she sits down beside* EILEEN.

TESSA: I think you should come and stay with us for a few days.

EILEEN: I won't, pet. The only way to get used to an empty house is to live in it.

A slight pause.

MATTY: I'll go, and come back, Mum.

TESSA: All right.

    MATTY *goes into the house.*

EILEEN: I'm glad it's this way round. He could do scrambled egg, and that was it.
    D'you think I stopped him dreaming, Tess?

TESSA: Of course not.

EILEEN: I did, you know.

A slight pause.

TESSA: Mum, I think your own doctor should write a death certificate. I'm not certain I can. Don't you worry about it, I'll ring him.

EILEEN: Will you?

TESSA: Yes.

EILEEN: Don't listen to 'im if 'e goes on about yer dad. It'll be stuff and nonsense.

TESSA: Dad came to me about his incontinence. It's very, very common, there's nothing to be ashamed of.

EILEEN: I didn't know that?

TESSA: He didn't want you worried.

EILEEN: I was worried.

TESSA: I know you were.

EILEEN: Then why didn't you tell me?

TESSA: He asked me not to.

EILEEN: Did he ring you?

TESSA: Yes. He came to the hospital. We looked at him properly.

EILEEN: I didn't know any of this, Tess.

A slight pause.

TESSA: I asked him to tell you, but he wouldn't.

EILEEN: Why?

TESSA: I don't know, Mum.

EILEEN: He was getting his own back, wasn't he?

TESSA: That's very silly.

EILEEN: Is it?

TESSA: You must know it is.

EILEEN: I don't.

A slight pause.

Jolly was very bitter, you know. He thought life had let him down.

TESSA: Did he?

EILEEN: He was very bitter. I'd be a fool if I didn't know that I was his life.

TESSA: I think you're twisting things, Mum.

EILEEN: Twisting what?

TESSA: Twisting your memories.

A slight pause.

When I was seven, Jolly was working. You've nothing to feel guilty about.

EILEEN: He wanted to study, you know. He always did. We couldn't afford it. All my life that's what I've said. When you went off to university, he shone like the sun. He said: I wanted Stephen to be the doctor, but now it's our Tess.

A slight pause.

I just worried you'd fall into bad company.

TESSA: I didn't, did I?

EILEEN: No, you've made your life very good. He was proud of you.

A slight pause.

He could always meet you, Tess. D'you know what I mean?

TESSA: Not really, I don't.

EILEEN: In intelligence, up here.

EILEEN *taps her head.*

I've wanted to say this for a long time. Not say, so much as admit. For most of my life I've been a very jealous woman.

TESSA: Mum –

EILEEN: If yer dad had been on his own – this is true, Tess – you'd have come home much more often. I've seen yer dad broken because you didn't come home.

TESSA *looks down, and then she looks back up.*

TESSA: Why don't we wait before we say these things?

EILEEN: I want you to understand that I do know what I'm like.

TESSA: Mum –

EILEEN: Jolly used to say that you make time for the things you really want to do. You didn't come home because of me. That is the truth, isn't it?

TESSA: I've had my career. And Matty. I've wanted him to grow up responsibly and strong.

EILEEN: Yes.

TESSA: It isn't you. Now isn't the time. Not for recrimination.

EILEEN: I'm worried there never will be a time. Yer dad used to say: our Tess has outgrown us, Eileen. I used to say: she's flown the nest, pet.

A slight pause.

If I was him sitting here you'd be telling him the truth, wouldn't you? I've always kept the truth away.

A slight pause.

He was such a dreamer. It was me who made the ends meet. I was busy running the family.

A slight pause.

I used to think: we'll not have a family if I let him dream – we'll be out on the streets – we'll be begging. Isn't that stupid? I'm sorry, Tess.

TESSA: It isn't stupid, Mum.

EILEEN: It is, you know.

A slight pause.

I suppose the one thing I've learnt – is that somehow you do get by. That must be true, because we did.

TESSA: Yes.

EILEEN: I am sorry.

TESSA: You've nothing to be sorry for.

EILEEN: I have, you know.

A slight pause.

TESSA: It's Dr Cottie, isn't it, Mum?

EILEEN: Mmm?

TESSA: Your doctor. Dr Cottie?

EILEEN: Yes, it is.

Scene Three

Later that day.

At the top of a sloping, shingle beach is a wooden sign saying: Tees Sailing Club. Below the sign is a lifebelt hanging onto a hook on the same pole. On the shingle is a G.P.14 sailing dinghy. It is standing on its metal launching trolley. Evening. It is very still. There are long shadows from the sun.

MATTY *is standing looking at the sea. He has the box under his arm, and white paint on his hands.*

JOLYON *is beside the boat. He is painting the hull with a brush and a pot of white paint. He has paint on his hands. He is wearing a white woodworking apron which gives him a slightly ghostly appearance.*

A slight pause.

MATTY: Can I ask you something, Grandpa?

JOLYON *paints.*

JOLYON: It depends what it is.

MATTY: Would you still marry Eileen?

JOLYON *paints.*

JOLYON: That's a question and a half, isn't it?

JOLYON *paints.*

MATTY *sits down. He takes an egg from the box and plays with it between his fingers.*

MATTY: But you learnt to love her, didn't you?

JOLYON: I think so. Yes.

JOLYON *paints.*

MATTY: That's all I wanted to know really.

JOLYON *paints.*

MATTY *runs the egg between his fingers.*

JOLYON *puts the brush on top of the paint pot.*

JOLYON: I must go. Nature calls again.

JOLYON *goes.*

MATTY *puts the egg back into the box. He stands up, goes to the boat, and puts the box on the bow. He picks up the paint brush and continues to paint.*

A pause.

TESSA *enters.*

MATTY: You were bloody mad.

TESSA: Who was mad?

MATTY *looks up.*

MATTY: Where did you come from?

TESSA: I've been searching high and low for you.

MATTY: I've been here, doing this.

TESSA *joins him.*

I was thinking about Grandpa, that was all.

TESSA: Why was he mad?

MATTY: Look in the dinghy.

TESSA *looks in the boat.*

MATTY *puts the brush on top of the paint pot. He takes a cardboard box from the boat. It is full of tinned and packet foods. He puts the box on the shingle, kneels, and takes from it tins of soup, meat, vegetables, and fruit. Eventually he upends the box and the rest of the tins and packets tumble out.*

He was stocking up. He was planning to sail to Russia.

TESSA: Matty, why didn't you tell me?

MATTY: He made me promise not to.

He stands up and takes another carboard box from the boat. He puts it down and kneels. He takes pots and pans, a tin-opener, and a portable gas-ring from it.

I think towards the end he was going senile. Was he, Mum?

TESSA: Where was he getting all this?

MATTY: He was buying it. It's all new.

TESSA *kneels.*

TESSA: He must've known what he was doing, didn't he? It was probably a little joke with himself.

MATTY: Some joke.

TESSA: Yes, I agree.

MATTY: Actually, I don't think it was. He was very serious about going to Russia.

He stands.

I've been trying to slow us down. I've been painting as badly as I could.

He takes two plastic water-carriers from the boat.

Then something else would appear.

TESSA: It's certainly perverse.

MATTY *kneels.*

MATTY: I think he was going.

TESSA: No, he wasn't.

MATTY: He was.

TESSA: No. He was getting his own back. In his own quiet way he was being a little bit spiteful.

MATTY: Spiteful?

TESSA: Yes.

MATTY: To who?

TESSA: To your grandmother, I think. To Eileen, probably.

MATTY: But I don't think she knows, Mum.

TESSA: No. I don't expect she does.

MATTY: How can it be spiteful then?

A slight pause.

TESSA: It was the way he learnt to cope with her. To wander off on his own periodically and do his own thing.

MATTY: Be perverse, you mean?

TESSA: It certainly looks like it, doesn't it?

MATTY: Yes. Why?

A slight pause.

TESSA: Oh, I suspect he felt bossed about. Eileen can be bossy, can't she?

MATTY: Sometimes.

TESSA: I suspect he occasionally felt stifled by her. And I don't blame him.

A slight pause.

MATTY: What d'you mean by stifled.

A slight pause.

TESSA: Oh, I think he wanted more from the world than just Eileen.

A slight pause.

MATTY: You feel like grandpa, don't you? About gran, I mean.

A slight pause.

I asked him if he'd still marry her?

TESSA: What was his reply?

MATTY: He said he thought so. Then nature called. We're a funny family.

TESSA: I asked him once. A long time ago.

MATTY: What did he say?

TESSA: He said: no.

A slight pause.

It was a weekend he came on his own to visit me at university.

MATTY: In London?

TESSA: Yes. Eileen was being particularly savage to him. He sat on my bed and cried.

MATTY: What about?

TESSA: It was actually about getting a television. Jolly would always spend money, if they had it. It seems strange now when you think how their life together revolved around the television.

MATTY: Yes.

TESSA: What was on it. What programmes they saw. They viewed the world from the television.

A slight pause.

MATTY: Is that what made Jolly bitter, Mum?

TESSA: What?

MATTY: I don't know really – seeing places like Russia – and not being able to go?

TESSA: I think it did make him bitter, yes.

MATTY *stands up.*

MATTY: Gran said he could go anywhere in this boat. He couldn't though, could he?

TESSA: No.

MATTY: He knew he couldn't, didn't he?

TESSA: Yes.

MATTY: He was just a poor old fucker who wanted to enjoy himself.

TESSA: Matty.

MATTY: He was though, wasn't he?

A slight pause.

TESSA: I think so, darling.

A slight pause.

We must be very, very careful with my mum during the next few weeks.

MATTY: Is she going to come and stay?

TESSA: No, she won't.

MATTY: Why?

TESSA: I suspect she's probably better off in her own home.

MATTY: You don't like her very much, do you, Mum?

A slight pause.

TESSA: Matty, I can't take much more of this. I came to find you because I thought you'd be a comfort.

A slight pause.

MATTY *goes to his mother, he touches her on the arm.*

MATTY: Would you like a drink? Mmm? I can go to the bar.

TESSA: Have you some money?

MATTY: I've got some.

MATTY *goes.*

A pause.

TESSA *stands up.*

MATTY *returns.*

They won't serve me. It's that horrible fat barman on.

TESSA: Have you even looked at any schoolwork this summer?

MATTY *shrugs.*

MATTY: I've been too busy.

TESSA: I thought not. What happened to that reading list you had, and the cheque I gave you?

MATTY: I put it in my deposit account.

TESSA: It won't buy a book there, will it?

MATTY: It's getting the interest.

TESSA: That's not the point.

MATTY: I will, Mum, don't worry.

TESSA: Yes, I've heard that before, too.

MATTY: Don't get at me, please. I'm very good when I want to be.

TESSA *smiles*.

TESSA: Yes, you are really.

MATTY: Actually, Mum, it's possible to buy them half price, from pupils who've just left.

TESSA: Doesn't that mean you wouldn't have them until the beginning of term?

MATTY: Well, not quite. Actually, they hold the sale at the end of term. Last term, I mean.

TESSA: So you've bought them already? You are a cheat, Matty.

MATTY: I only bought one or two. Not all of them.

TESSA: Where are they?

MATTY: I left them at school.

TESSA: Had you no intention of doing any work?

MATTY: I'm going to read the ones I have to buy here. I thought I'd better tell you, that was all.

TESSA: Yes. I'm not sure I approve.

MATTY: It seemed sensible, don't you think?

TESSA: I expect so.

MATTY: They're only for reading round the subject. It's just better to have your own.

TESSA: You don't need to convince me.

MATTY: Thanks, Mum.

TESSA *smiles*.

I'm sorry about just now – you know – being unfeeling and things.

TESSA: I was very fond of him.

MATTY: I thought I might try and write a pamphlet about Grandpa. Like those thirties pamphlets of his.

TESSA: A pamphlet?

MATTY: It wouldn't be very good. I don't mean to be big-headed.

TESSA *smiles*.

A history, sort of thing – about how the eggs might have come from Russia. Don't you think it's a good idea?

TESSA: It's very good.

MATTY: Don't patronize me, Mum.

TESSA: I wasn't. It is a good idea.

MATTY: I had a look in the library and I think the most likely way was with a trade delegation – the mysterious Russian must have been an entrepreneur. I thought I'd start with that.

TESSA *smiles*.

TESSA: I'm sorry, darling, I'm just very tired. I've had a difficult afternoon with Eileen.

MATTY: Is she all right?

TESSA: Not really. I don't know what to do. I wonder if we shouldn't go now, and insist she comes back with us?

MATTY *shrugs.*

MATTY: If she doesn't want to come –

TESSA: She keeps going on about it being an empty house.

A slight pause.

MATTY: I don't know, I'm not an expert. Have they taken him?

TESSA: Yes, the undertaker's been.

MATTY: So his body's not there?

TESSA: No. We did all that very well.

MATTY: Did you really have to wash him?

TESSA: Yes.

MATTY: I don't know how you could. (*He has pulled a face.*)

TESSA: All the neighbours know.

MATTY *kneels. He begins to put the tins and pans back into their boxes.*

I think what we'll do is call in, Matty. If you don't mind?

MATTY: No.

TESSA: Suggest she comes for the evening, and then I'll run her home if she doesn't want to stay.

MATTY: Yes.

TESSA: I suspect if we get her there, she will.

MATTY: I think that's best, too.

TESSA: Do you?

MATTY: I've just said so, Mum.

TESSA: We'd better take all this with us. No, we hadn't, we'd better leave it in the boat.

TESSA *helps* MATTY.

MATTY *lifts the boxes and the water-carriers into the boat.*

MATTY: It probably would've sunk anyway – all this stuff in it.

TESSA: Where did he say he was sailing to?

MATTY: Siberia.

TESSA: It's not on the sea.

MATTY: I know.

TESSA: And you took him seriously?

MATTY: Well, I didn't, not quite. If you're thinking of sailing to Siberia it doesn't really matter whether it's on the sea or not, does it?

TESSA *smiles.*

TESSA: Poor you.

MATTY *takes the box from the bow of the boat and gives it to* TESSA *to hold. He puts the lid on the pot of paint.*

I haven't seen you using the easel?

MATTY *puts the paint pot into the boat. He finds a jar of turpentine, and puts the brush in that.*

MATTY: I thought I might sell it.

TESSA: Have you used it at all, Matty?

MATTY *takes a green canvas cover from inside the boat. He begins to fit it, first at the stern, and then at the bow.*

MATTY: Well, not really, Mum. I haven't had much time.

TESSA: It isn't good enough, you know.

MATTY: Well, I thought if I sold it – it is a good idea, don't you think?

TESSA: No, I don't.

A slight pause.

MATTY: I have other things I need much more.

TESSA: It was a very expensive easel and you're absolutely not going to sell it. Have I made myself plain?

A slight pause.

MATTY: I think we should at least consider it.

TESSA: Matty.

MATTY: What?

TESSA: Shut up.

A slight pause.

MATTY: Well, I thought if we sold it we could buy a printer for the computer. I'm mainly thinking of you – you know how you're always grumbling.

TESSA: Matty.

MATTY: What?

TESSA: I have said 'no'.

MATTY: Oh, don't be silly. You're always saying we need a printer.

TESSA: I have never said that.

MATTY: You have, Mum.

TESSA: Matty.

MATTY: What?

TESSA: One more word and I'll clout you. Is that clear?

MATTY *stops, he looks up at her.*

MATTY: It isn't very fair. I'm only doing my best, you know.

TESSA: I know you do your best.

MATTY: Well then –

TESSA: No.

MATTY: Oh, Mum.

TESSA: This time it's no, darling. You're getting away with far too much.

MATTY: Me?

TESSA: Matty, if you don't shut up I'll take back the money you made on those school books.

MATTY *continues to fit the canvas cover.*

MATTY: What's come over you?

TESSA: Nothing.

MATTY: Is it my fault?

A slight pause.

Is it Jolly?

TESSA: No, darling, it's you. You're becoming a manipulater, and I'm not having it.

MATTY *stops, he looks up.*

MATTY: You can do this on your own then. I'm going.

MATTY *goes.*

A slight pause.

TESSA *walks to the boat. She continues to fit the canvas cover.*

Scene Four

Tees Sailing Club. A hot late August afternoon.

The G.P.14 sailing dinghy is painted and varnished. Its cover is off. Nearby, on a thin pole pushed into the shingle, is a cardboard sign saying: For sale.

MATTY, *wearing a t-shirt, is standing one side of the dinghy.*

EILEEN, *wearing a cotton dress, is standing the other. Nearby is a picnic basket.*

MATTY: We did a good job, don't you think?

EILEEN: Yes, she looks lovely.

MATTY: We had her stripped right down. Well, grandpa did most of it.

EILEEN: Jolly built her himself.

MATTY: I know. From a kit.

EILEEN: That's right. One summer. In our backyard. Come the end of August he had to knock part of a wall down to get her out. It was a terrible palaver. The whole road came out, it was such a sight. Then half of them wanted a go. A sail. So Jolly took them out, one by one. Most of them faded away when they realised it meant gettin' yer bum all wet.

She smiles.

When we were racing, Matty, he'd always want to win, so you got hollered at as well. I said to him once: why can't we come second, Jolly? Second wasn't in his nature.

MATTY: Did he win?

EILEEN: Most often he did. It was the sheer joy 'e got from it. He never settled, you know, when he got too old to sail. He missed it like anything. I know he did. Jolly wasn't a spectator.

MATTY: Is she worth any less because she was built from a kit?

EILEEN: I don't see why.

MATTY: You must make sure you get more than they offer.

EILEEN: Isn't a thing worth what someone will pay for it?

MATTY: I'm just warning you.

EILEEN: I don't need warning, thank you.

MATTY: I'd ask for at least a hundred pounds more.

EILEEN: Yes, well –

MATTY: It's the way business is done.

EILEEN: Is it? In that case I might leave it up to you. He'll probably take one look at you and think: here's a silly boy, I can get it a hundred pounds cheaper.

MATTY: That isn't very fair.

EILEEN: Don't you answer me back either.

MATTY: I wasn't. I was thinking of you.

EILEEN: I will get what is right. You're far too quick to jump on to money.

MATTY (*quietly, turning away*): Yes, Gran. Three bags full, Gran.

EILEEN (*going to him*): Now, I didn't mean to spoil our day. So let's forget it, shall we?

TESSA enters wearing a summer dress. She is carrying three drinks: a light ale, a vodka and orange, and a half pint of lager.

TESSA: I've told them that if anyone asks, we're down here.

MATTY takes the lager from her.

MATTY: Thanks, Mum.

EILEEN takes the light ale.

EILEEN: It feels like a holiday to be having a drink. Thank you. I will get us one later.

PAVEL enters.

PAVEL is a tall, slightly stocky man of fifty-nine, whose hair is receding. He is wearing a dark suit, a tie, and a white shirt.

PAVEL stops.

PAVEL: Mrs Davis?

TESSA: This is Mrs Davis.

PAVEL steps forward.

PAVEL: Dear lady, my name is Professor Pavel Kabalevsky, I am the director of the Oka nature reserve.

A slight pause.

I am so sorry if I have interrupted you.

A slight pause.

TESSA: No, it's all right.

PAVEL (*to TESSA*): I have called at this lady's house, but no, she is not there, you understand me?

TESSA: Yes.

PAVEL (*to EILEEN*): A neighbour of yours, I think, she says you are here, so here I come following the road. She says sometimes you are at home, and sometimes with your daughter. My time here is very short, I have only one day, you understand me?

EILEEN: Yes.

PAVEL: It is urgent for me. Then I must go to Baraboo, Wisconsin, America. But I am so excited by this letter, dear lady, it is the greatest excitement.

EILEEN: Yes.

PAVEL takes the letter from the inside pocket of his jacket.

PAVEL: This letter, you know, it is waiting for me at the BBC in Bristol. I go to

Bristol before going to Baraboo, Wisconsin, America. I talk with the BBC, maybe, about making another film. But I do not know. I do not think so now. It cost so much money, you understand me?

EILEEN: I understand.

PAVEL: Good. So I am here and I would like it very much to meet your husband.

EILEEN: Yes.

A slight pause.

PAVEL: My time here is very short. Only one day.

TESSA: I'm Mrs Davis's daughter.

PAVEL: It is a pleasure to meet you all.

MATTY: I'm Matthew.

PAVEL: How do you all do.

PAVEL *shakes hands with them.*

Now I would like it very much to meet Mr Davis.

TESSA: Mr Davis died a fortnight ago.

A slight pause.

PAVEL: He is not here?

He turns to EILEEN.

I am so sorry. For you, dear lady, I am so very sorry.

EILEEN: He passed away very suddenly, didn't he?

TESSA: Yes.

MATTY: After he'd written to you. Mr Davis wanted to go to Russia.

A slight pause.

PAVEL: I was intrigued by his letter, you understand me? The White Siberian Crane it is nearly all my life for over ten years. I criss-cross the world in my endeavour to return this bird to his natural place. We are on the very brink of success. This letter, somehow, it make me think about what has gone before, you understand me? This is why I come. I think this man – Mr Davis – he has a part of my history, somehow. You understand?

EILEEN: Yes.

PAVEL: I am not the relation he thinks. I do not know these other people he writes to me about. It is not for that reason I come, you understand?

EILEEN: Yes.

PAVEL: But I like to meet the man who has these eggs. I want to ask him if he loves the birds as I do. I think so from his letter. That I like very much. My desire is a very simple one.

EILEEN: Yes.

A slight pause.

PAVEL: But I have interrupted you, dear people.

TESSA: No. Would you like a drink?

PAVEL: I would like very much a pint of your English bitter, please. Thank you.

TESSA *puts her glass on the bow of the boat.*

Your English pubs fascinate me.

TESSA *smiles and goes.*

When I am with the BBC we go into pubs all the time for discussions.

EILEEN: I remember you from the television.

PAVEL: Sometimes I am so nervous I get wrong what I have to say, and they shout 'cut', and we have to start again.

MATTY: Are you making another programme?

PAVEL: I have tried to say I do not think so. I am very disappointed by this. I look for a way of telling my story, you understand. These birds are very important.

EILEEN: We enjoyed it.

PAVEL: Thank you. It is shown in the Soviet Union, too. We, too, have our wildlife programmes for people to be educated about ecology. This is most important.

MATTY: How did they film it?

PAVEL: They come to my home. I live in the little village of Brukin Bor, which is on the Pra river. This is the centre of the Oka nature reserve. At first they do the background. They ask the local children to be jolly in the river for them. This they shoot. And the women drawing water from the well, too. We always hear a cry of 'hair in the gate'. So, like 'cut', everyone has to do it again. By now the children are blue. The Pra river is very cold in April. It made me laugh, you know, because they are blue and shivering, and getting them to take a hot bath is sometimes difficult. Mothers, I think, must make a camera, and say 'turn over' when it is bath-time. But this you saw on the film, dear lady?

EILEEN: Yes.

PAVEL: We are fascinated to have this camera in our lives.

EILEEN: Television's a wonderful thing, isn't it?

PAVEL: I think this is so.

MATTY: How long were they were?

PAVEL: For three weeks. Once the women have drawn the water from the well, and the cart has come along the lane, and the man has ridden his motorbike over the humps, and the boy has tethered his grandfather's cow, and girl has chased her chickens – then we go into the Oka reserve to film the wildlife. The wildlife there is very special for me. I dream of the day I see the White Siberian Crane.

TESSA *enters with a pint of bitter.* PAVEL *puts the letter back in his pocket and takes his drink.*

I must thank you, dear lady. I must thank you all for being so kind already.

He drinks some beer.

This, it is delicious.

MATTY: Why are you going to America?

PAVEL: It is here, now, in America, that there is a flock of Siberian Cranes. Ten years ago we have taken four eggs from the north of Siberia. In Baraboo, Wisconsin, they have hatched these rare eggs, and raised the chicks by hand. These chicks are now mature, and they are laying eggs of their own. I must go to prepare. This spring they will take these eggs. I, myself, will go once more to America. In an incubator I will carry the eggs back to the Oka reserve. There, we will go deep into the forests, and we will put them on to the nest of the Grey Crane. He is very common, not so special. You understand the cuckoo, dear people?

MATTY: Yes.

PAVEL: We hope the Grey Crane will be a cuckoo for the Siberian Crane eggs. He will hatch, and raise the chicks as his own. In this way, we save this bird from extinction. If we are successful he will go on growing in the wild. I am very optimistic now.

PAVEL *smiles. He drinks some beer.*

TESSA: When do you go back to the Soviet Union?

PAVEL: I have one week only in America. I miss my family very much. Unfortunately it is not possible for them to accompany me, you understand? My son he is only fourteen. He has his school and must do well at that.

He smiles.

Also, my English, it is taught to me by my wife. My wife, she is from England many years ago. This makes it doubly difficult for me to travel. I have many difficulties at first. They want to know everything. It took me eight years. I am very privileged.

He smiles.

My wife, she is brought up in Royal Tunbridge Wells. I go there, too, for one day only. I like to see the streets she played in. I say to her: I know what Tunbridge Wells is like now. And she laughs, you know.

EILEEN: Would you like to share our picnic?

PAVEL: I know about English picnicking. I would like that very much.

MATTY *puts his lager on the bow of the boat. He takes the green canvas cover from inside and begins to spread it on the shingle.*

TESSA *helps him.*

Is this your boat?

EILEEN: Yes.

PAVEL: Where I live we have boats, too. I live on the flood plain of the Oka river. In spring the forests are deep in water. When the snow melts, you understand me?

EILEEN: Yes.

PAVEL: I would like it very much to see these eggs if this is possible?

EILEEN: Matty has them.

PAVEL: May I ask if he is your grandchild?

EILEEN: Yes, he is.

PAVEL: He reminds me of my own boy a little. Always helpful, I think?

EILEEN (*smiling*): Yes.

PAVEL: Good boys.

EILEEN: Matty, what happened to the eggs?

MATTY: They're at home unfortunately.

PAVEL: Such a pity. Another time, perhaps?

EILEEN: Yes.

PAVEL: He works hard at school, I hope?

EILEEN: I think so. Don't you?

MATTY: Sometimes.

PAVEL: Ah, but, sometimes is not enough.

EILEEN: He won't be bossed about.

PAVEL: That is just like my son. Independent people.

The canvas cover is spread across the shingle.

EILEEN *picks up the picnic basket. They sit down around it.*

EILEEN *begins to unwrap the packages of tinfoil, and spread the picnic. There are sandwiches, cakes and pieces of fruit.*

Dear people, this is the nicest day I have spent in England.

TESSA: When do you leave for America?

PAVEL: I must go tomorrow morning.

MATTY: He can stay with us, can't he?

TESSA: Would you like to stay with us this evening?

PAVEL: I have checked into a hotel. But I will cancel it. Thank you very much.

EILEEN *gives them all a paper serviette.*

EILEEN: I didn't bother with plates. There's egg and tomato, cheese, and some chicken.

She takes a bag from the basket.

And one or two extra tomatoes here. You'll have to all dive in and help yourselves.

PAVEL: Mr Davis, he was an ornithologist?

A slight pause.

TESSA: Mum, was dad an ornithologist?

EILEEN: No, he just happened to have the eggs. It was seeing you on the television that reminded him.

PAVEL *smiles.*

PAVEL: Was it his hobby?

EILEEN: It wasn't even as much as that.

PAVEL: But he was interested a little?

EILEEN: Yes.

PAVEL: I wonder if maybe he is an ornithologist, you know. It is his friend Aram he is interested in? I understand now.

EILEEN: There was nothing special about Jolly.

PAVEL: Except, of course, to you, dear lady.

EILEEN: I think if you don't mind I'm going to go for a little walk.

She stands up.

I won't be very long. Help yourselves, won't you?

TESSA *stands.*

TESSA: I'll come with you, Mum.

PAVEL *stands.*

EILEEN: I'd rather go on my own, Tess.

TESSA: Are you sure?

EILEEN: Yes. Dig in and I won't be long.

EILEEN *goes.*

PAVEL: It is very frightening when we lose someone so close to us. I must thank you all for your hospitality, but I must go, too. I do not like to be the cause of this lady being frightened.

TESSA: No. Stay.

MATTY: It's me, Mum. I upset her earlier.

TESSA: Matty. Honestly.

MATTY: I didn't mean to. I'm sick of watching my p's and q's.

PAVEL: If I go to my hotel, dear people, perhaps I may meet you all this evening?

TESSA: Stay. Please.

MATTY: Shall I go after her?

TESSA: No.

PAVEL: I am worried about this lady.

TESSA: There's nothing to worry about.

PAVEL: I am still worried.

MATTY: She didn't expect you, did she, Mum?

TESSA: No.

PAVEL: I do somethings and I surprise myself sometimes.

PAVEL *sits down.*

TESSA: I'll just go and catch her up.

TESSA *goes after* EILEEN.

PAVEL: You know, I think when we are older, the world it begins to go a little faster than us.

MATTY: Yes.

A slight pause.

PAVEL: You know, now that I begin to travel and see the world, I realise so much more.

MATTY: Do you?

PAVEL: Of course. I begin to realise just how fast the world is. We are so easily left behind.

A slight pause.

If I am a shock for her – but you must tell me if this is true about your grandmother?

TESSA *enters.*

TESSA: She's very upset. She just runs away.

TESSA *sits.*

PAVEL: If it is me, please tell me?

TESSA: It is, yes.

PAVEL: I am so very sorry.

TESSA: My father would've loved to have visited your country. That's all it is.

PAVEL: It is because I am here?

TESSA: She feels guilty.

A slight pause.

PAVEL: I think I must go.

TESSA: No. Stay.

PAVEL: If I upset her?

TESSA: It doesn't matter.

MATTY: It does her good.

TESSA: That's a horrible thing to say.

MATTY: You've said it.

A slight pause.

TESSA: I'm sorry to involve you in our squabbles.

EILEEN *enters.*

MATTY: Are you all right, Gran?

EILEEN: I will be in a minute. You haven't even started. Aren't you hungry, Mr Kabalevsky?

PAVEL *stands.*

PAVEL: You must forgive me, dear lady.

EILEEN: I'm the one making a fool of myself.

She joins them.

It's very good of you to come and visit us.

PAVEL: I was worried, you know.

EILEEN: You don't have to worry about me.

EILEEN *sits.*

You've come a long way, haven't you?

PAVEL: It is not so very far from Bristol.

PAVEL *sits.*

EILEEN: I was meaning from Russia, Mr Kabalevsky.

PAVEL: The Soviet Union is a vast country, if you understand me? So many different people, so many distances.

EILEEN: Do we seem small here?

PAVEL: In my country it is a privilege to travel. You are very lucky.

EILEEN: I bet we must seem small really.

PAVEL *smiles.*

PAVEL: A little. You know, it is so easy to travel around England. Even I manage this easily.

EILEEN: That's more than me, Mr Kabalevsky.

PAVEL: You do not travel so much?

EILEEN: No. We would've liked to. It came too late for us.

PAVEL: I understand. It is much the same. Do you think it is the young people who will have these things?

EILEEN: I do. An' good on them for it. I hope they learn something from it.

PAVEL: I think it is the young people, too.

A slight pause.

EILEEN: I didn't make this for it to go all dry.

They begin to eat the large picnic.

What d'you think about responsibility, Mr Kabalevsky?

PAVEL: I beg your pardon, dear lady?

EILEEN: It's crossed my mind that the more people have, the less responsible they are.

PAVEL *thinks*.

PAVEL: Yes, responsibility to one's country is most important. We must all work together for the same ideals.

MATTY: What d'you like best about England?

PAVEL: I have tried to say I think it is your freedom to travel. My son, he is fourteen. I hope he will travel, too, one day very soon. I would like him to be like you, always helpful to his family.

EILEEN *smiles*.

EILEEN: Matty's been abroad, haven't you?

MATTY: I've been to Greece and Portugal. And America. I went there with Mum when my father emigrated.

PAVEL: My son, Nikolai, would love to talk with you. He is very fond of people.

PAVEL *smiles*.

Why do you only sometimes work hard at school?

A slight pause.

MATTY: Well, I was joking mainly.

TESSA: He doesn't like to be thought of as a swot.

PAVEL: A swot? Does this mean you are being modest to me?

MATTY: Well, not really. A little, perhaps.

PAVEL: But I like to see modesty in young people. It is best for them.

MATTY: I try to be.

PAVEL: You like your school very much?

MATTY: Yes.

PAVEL: It is near here? But you are on your summer holiday.

MATTY: I attend St Peter's School in York.

TESSA: He boards at a public school.

PAVEL: Ah. You are very privileged?

MATTY: Yes.

EILEEN: Matty's very lucky.

PAVEL: I understand.

A slight pause.

Dear lady, when you talk about responsibility, are you talking about the responsibility of knowing how lucky you are?

EILEEN: Yes, I am.

PAVEL: Ah. I understand you now.

PAVEL *smiles*.

You know, I think the world it will belong to you young people. You must be very wise with it. I would like you very much to meet my son.

MATTY *puts down his sandwich*.

MATTY: Mum.

TESSA: Are you inviting him, Mr Kabalevsky?

PAVEL: I am, yes. I think we must see if this is possible.

EILEEN: Would you like to go, Matty?

MATTY: Me? You must be joking. Of course I would.

PAVEL: You would enjoy seeing the White Siberian Crane?

MATTY: Yes, not half.

PAVEL: Good. I will speak with some people I know.

MATTY: I'd love it.

EILEEN: What does he have t'do?

PAVEL: Nothing for the moment. Please, you must leave this with me. Very often I am quite lucky. But I will have to fight for it. I am a fighter, you know. All my life I have been a fighter.

   PAVEL, EILEEN *and* TESSA *are looking at* MATTY.

Scene Five

Later. Early evening.

A vast lawn. A single apple tree which is laden with apples. A grass rake is leaning against the tree.

A bright sun.

EILEEN *is standing by herself.*

TESSA *enters. She is smoking a cigarette.*

EILEEN: I'm coming.

TESSA: There's no hurry, I've only just put the potatoes on.

   TESSA *joins* EILEEN.

EILEEN: I'd like to tell you something, Tess.

TESSA: What?

EILEEN: Watt invented steam.

TESSA: I walked into that, didn't I? Mum, what d'you want to tell me? Is it important or not?

EILEEN: I was looking at the garden, thinking about Matty.

TESSA: I know he isn't perfect, Mum, but he's all I have. Yes?

EILEEN: I know that, pet. We're so much at cross-purposes you and me.

TESSA: We're at cross-purposes, Mum, because you will interfere. Until you learn to leave well alone we will be.

   A slight pause.

EILEEN: That's put me in my place.

TESSA: Stop being bloody manipulative. You're as bad as Matty.

EILEEN: I know.

TESSA: Mum, if you know, why the hell do you carry on? At least he has sixteen as an excuse.

   A slight pause.

EILEEN: All my life I feel I've been in the middle of battles.

A slight pause.

Battles for this, battles f'that. Battles to keep our heads above water. I'm so jealous of him, Tess. That's what I wanted to tell you.

She is really upset. TESSA *hugs her.*

TESSA: Oh, Mum.

EILEEN: It's easier to think the right thoughts than it is to do the right things.

She is crying.

MATTY *enters.*

MATTY: Mum, Mr Kabalevsky would – like – to – see.

TESSA: I'll come and find you later, darling.

MATTY: Yes.

MATTY *goes.*

EILEEN: He has the world at his feet. I just hope he succeeds, because I haven't. All my life I've been battling. Battling for you. Battling for Jolly. Battling for what is right. An' all I feel is a failure. Because if you look at the world all you see is greed. I'm very jealous of greedy people. I wish I was.

TESSA: Mum –

EILEEN: No, it's true, Tess. I don't mean you and Matty because you're family. I really don't. You'll have to believe me.

TESSA: I do.

EILEEN: I've always loved you all, you know.

TESSA: I know.

EILEEN: I've always wanted the best for you all. You've had the best, Tess. And we struggled for it I can tell you.

TESSA: I know, Mum. Don't be upset.

EILEEN: I can't help it. I'm like a coil at the moment.

TESSA: Listen, if you're worried about Matty being greedy and selfish – don't. He's my responsibility, isn't he?

EILEEN: He seems to get everything he wants, Tess. It isn't right.

TESSA: Mum, he doesn't actually.

EILEEN: Doesn't he?

TESSA: No. He's growing up. He's got to be allowed to grow up.

EILEEN: I think that's what I mean, love. What's he going to be like when he's older?

TESSA: Matty's very sensitive, Mum. He isn't stupid. In any case he's my responsibility. Not yours.

EILEEN: I can't help feeling partly responsible.

TESSA: You mustn't.

EILEEN: No.

A slight pause.

I expect I've got everything jumbled up.

EILEEN *breaks the hug.* TESSA *takes her hand.*

TESSA: You haven't. You're doing what you think is proper. I'm very grateful.

EILEEN: Oh, I don't know, love. I ought to know better at my age.

TESSA: Mum, it's time you enjoyed yourself. My problems, Matty's problems, they're not of your making. Are they?

EILEEN: No. Why do I feel so guilty then?

TESSA: You mustn't carry us on your shoulders.

EILEEN: No.

A slight pause.

I used to think living was so simple. It isn't, is it? Mind you, I think it used to be simpler. I don't envy Matty in a way.

A slight pause.

I think you're right – I must just try an' enjoy myself a bit more.

TESSA: You must.

EILEEN: You won't tell him what I've said, will you?

TESSA: Of course I won't.

EILEEN: It's all right f'me to know what a stupid woman I am – I don't want him to know it as well.

TESSA: He doesn't. You're not stupid.

EILEEN: Oh, I am.

TESSA: Mum, don't knock yourself so much.

EILEEN: I can't help it. It's the way I was brought up. I think what I'm jealous of is Matty's confidence.

EILEEN *has tears in her eyes.* TESSA *hugs her.*

TESSA: Come on, let's have no more.

A slight pause.

You were very confident with me when I was a child. I remember.

EILEEN: If I was it was all show. I didn't feel it. An' Stephen being killed like that. Why wasn't I watching him?

TESSA: You couldn't be everywhere, Mum. It wasn't your fault. You've done enough for other people. These things are in the past. Think about yourself for a change.

EILEEN: I'm going to wear myself out, Tess.

TESSA: I know you are. You mustn't. You're very important. There's only so much one person can do.

A slight pause.

Mum, I can't treat every patient in the hospital, can I? Can I, Mum?

EILEEN: No, you can't, love.

TESSA: You're asking Herculean things of yourself. It isn't fair. You must learn to let events ride sometimes.

EILEEN: What gets to me is being jealous. I don't understand it.

TESSA: You're not jealous, Mum. You're just worrying. You're worrying far too much. There's nothing to worry about.

EILEEN: No.

EILEEN *breaks the hug.*

A lot of this comes from Jolly. I miss him like a massive space was gone.

TESSA: I know. We all do. But he wouldn't want you to go around saying you were jealous, and all those things, would he?

EILEEN: I think I am a bit jealous, pet.

TESSA: Well, whatever you are, it doesn't matter. What matters is the future.

EILEEN: Yes.

TESSA: Think of something you've always wanted to do. And try and do that. And don't worry about it.

EILEEN: Yes.

TESSA: Is there something you wished you'd done, and never have?

EILEEN: There must be a million things.

TESSA: Don't worry about money.

EILEEN: There is one thing, pet.

TESSA: What?

EILEEN: He invented steam. I'm very jealous of Matty going to Russia.

ACT TWO

Scene One

The small garden adjoining a wooden house at the village of Brukin Bor in the Soviet Union. A mild afternoon the following late April.

The garden has a very low (perhaps no more than six-inches high) wooden fence around it with an opening for people to come in and out. It is painted blue but the harsh winter has cracked and taken much of the life from it. Along one side of the fence is a large, neatly stacked pile of cut logs. In one or two places a slushy snow is still on the muddy ground. Everywhere is damp and drab as spring slowly thaws the earth, and nothing has much colour.

MARGARET is sitting in the garden on a wooden chair. She has a workbasket beside her and she is darning a sock.

MARGARET is a thin woman of fifty-four. She is wearing stout shoes, a skirt and a blouse, and a cotton shawl around her shoulders.

MARGARET puts her darning into the workbasket and stands up.

NIKOLAI enters with EILEEN and MATTY. MATTY has a new rucksack on his back. NIKOLAI is carrying a case.

NIKOLAI is a small, thin, wiry, light-haired boy of fourteen. He speaks almost faultless English. He is wearing his school uniform with the red scarf of the Young Pioneers.

MATTY is wearing walking boots and a new, bright, expensive anorak. EILEEN is wearing stout shoes and a heavy coat.

MARGARET walks out of the garden to meet them on the muddy lane.

MARGARET: Welcome to Brukin Bor.

NIKOLAI: I would like you to meet my mother.

MARGARET: You must be Eileen.

    MARGARET and EILEEN shake hands.

    And Matty.

MATTY: Yes.

    MARGARET and MATTY shake hands.

MARGARET: Welcome.

MATTY: Thank you very much.

MARGARET: It's such a pleasure to have you come and visit us.

MATTY: It's wonderful to be here.

MARGARET: Nikolai's been meeting every bus for the last two days.

NIKOLAI: I am the talk of my school.

MARGARET: You are, aren't you?

NIKOLAI: Yes.

MARGARET (*to* EILEEN, *smiling*): I'm not a real English person. His schoolfriends are terribly impressed. I hope he wasn't too effusive at the bus-stop?

EILEEN: No, he was lovely.

MATTY: He recognised us straight away.

MARGARET: Come through into the garden.

They go through the opening.

MARGARET *takes the case from* NIKOLAI.

Why don't you take Matty to the den.

NIKOLAI: Come. Come with me.

MARGARET: Wait a minute, let me explain first. My husband has an office and, if you don't mind, I'd like you to share that with Nikolai?

MATTY: Yes.

MARGARET: We've put two campbeds there, and a little chest for your clothes.

MATTY: I can keep them in my rucksack.

MARGARET: That's up to you. Nikolai will help sort you out. It's not very far, but there's no water. So when you want a shower, or to wash at night, you'll have to do that here.

MATTY: Yes.

MARGARET: There's a stove, so you'll be nice and cosy. And I've told Nikolai that I don't want you staying up all night. It's all right to chat for half an hour, but after that I think it should be sleep.

MATTY: Yes.

MARGARET: Off you go the pair of you.

NIKOLAI: Come with me, Matty.

NIKOLAI *and* MATTY *go.*

MARGARET *and* EILEEN *smile at one another.*

MARGARET: I've put you in Nikolai's room.

EILEEN: You mustn't let us be a nuisance.

MARGARET: No, he's been longing to sleep in the den. You must know what growing boys are?

EILEEN *smiles.*

Would you like to have a wash? And I'll show you his bed.

EILEEN: In a minute.

MARGARET *smiles.*

MARGARET: Would you like a few moments on your own?

EILEEN: Yes, please.

MARGARET: I'll take your case in. Do come and find me when you're ready.

EILEEN: Thank you.

MARGARET *goes into the house.*

A pause.

EILEEN *follows her in.*

MARGARET *returns. She is carrying a wooden chair which she puts down. She waits.*

EILEEN *enters. She has her coat over her arm.*

MARGARET: If you don't mind he'll just need to pop in last thing at night.

EILEEN *smiles.*

EILEEN: He can come in whenever 'e wants.

MARGARET: I won't have him doing that.

EILEEN: Is he your only child?

MARGARET: No, we've two who are grown up. They're both well into their twenties now. Nikolai was rather a surprise.

EILEEN: Do the others come home?

MARGARET: Yes. As often as they can. Edvard works at Bratsk in Siberia so it's sometimes quite difficult. But when they do, they sleep in the den. My daughter's in Leningrad.

EILEEN: Is it easier for her?

MARGARET: Yes, she gets a train to Moscow. And then like you, a train from Moscow, and then the bus. Whereas Edvard only receives one aeroplane ticket a year. I write every week. Nikolai wants to be like his elder brother in the den. He'll only be popping in for underclothes and socks.

EILEEN: I don't mind at all.

MARGARET *smiles*.

MARGARET: My husband is still in America. I haven't any firm news. He agreed to telephone when he was sure he'd at least one fertile egg. I hope you can bear the uncertainty.

EILEEN: Yes.

MARGARET: I'm having to remind Nikolai there is a chance there won't be any. How would Matty react if that happened?

EILEEN: He'd be disappointed.

MARGARET: Would he?

EILEEN: He's his heart set on seeing them. Matty's ever an optimist. You can't knock him down.

MARGARET *smiles*.

MARGARET: He's like my husband. He's travelled to America with such high hopes.

EILEEN: Are you worried?

MARGARET: I know how vulnerable children are.

EILEEN: Don't worry on Matty's account.

MARGARET: Matty's being here is very important to Pavel.

EILEEN: Is it?

MARGARET: He's set great store by your both coming.

EILEEN: It's important t'me. I feel humbled as a matter of fact. Mebbe it's important t'say jus' now how grateful we are. Matty thinks it, but 'e might forget.

MARGARET: Is he an independent boy?

EILEEN: I have thought it's uncanny – in Moscow he hardly put a foot wrong. How he knew where we were going I'll never know. I kept looking at him and thinking: well, 'e could be Russian, he's so good at this. The only thing 'e didn't manage was rooms side by side in the hotel. But he tried.

She smiles.

I've been coming to the conclusion that the world is a small place to 'im. He either doesn't know how big the world is, or he doesn't care. Don't get me wrong, I think it's marvellous that he can get us here.

MARGARET: Is he as bright at school?

EILEEN: I'm told he is. He doesn't concentrate like 'e should. But children don't these days, do they? He's like a frog from one thing t'the other. You say that, yet he manages himself so well.

A slight pause.

What happens if there aren't any fertile eggs?

MARGARET: My husband will try again next year.

EILEEN: Do your other two children take an interest?

MARGARET: Yes, very much so.

EILEEN: It's good when families can do that, isn't it?

MARGARET *indicates a chair.*

MARGARET: Nikolai is growing up with all this excitement surrounding him, so it's rather different. Edvard and Rafiya didn't see their father travelling abroad. Nikolai is very special to my husband. He calls him our little miracle.

EILEEN *sits in the chair and puts her coat over her lap.*

EILEEN: Children are miracles, aren't they?

MARGARET: I'm very impressed with Matty.

MARGARET *sits.*

EILEEN: In Moscow I had to keep saying: pinch me, pinch me. I have never in my life seen so many people. You just get carried along with them, don't you?

MARGARET: A great deal of the excitement is the preparation for May Day, which is on Friday.

EILEEN: Is that what all the red is for?

MARGARET *smiles.*

MARGARET: You are here at an interesting time.

EILEEN *smiles.*

EILEEN: You know, the biggest shock was to see ordinary people going about their business. Getting onto trains, going to work. Getting into trams, coming home again. I know I must be ridiculous, am I?

MARGARET *smiles.*

And everything in Moscow is so massive, isn't it?

MARGARET: Yes, it is.

EILEEN: It was like having a telescope in front of my eyes. It was all closer for me. Mebbe that's daft?

MARGARET: No.

EILEEN: D'you like living here?

MARGARET: I like the Oka reserve. I'm not a Moscow person, no.

EILEEN: You have the space, don't you?

MARGARET: Yes.

A slight pause.

I enjoyed Tunbridge Wells. The journeys in the car. On Sunday. With my parents. When I was in my teens.

MARGARET *smiles.*

That life ended when I didn't choose to fall in love.

EILEEN: Didn't you?

MARGARET: Love finds us, I suspect. It found me in a very odd place. At first I was terribly reticent.

EILEEN: Yes.

MARGARET: Not unlike you, perhaps? I don't know. I felt this country was very different from my own.

A slight pause.

EILEEN: We didn't fall in love like that. It's good to see a woman who doesn't have regrets. You don't, do you?

MARGARET: No.

EILEEN: I married Jolly to get away from my mother. She was a tartar. I thought if we married I could live with his family.

MARGARET: Did you?

EILEEN: Yes. It was easy, you see, because I told Jolly I was pregnant by him. In actual fact it was another boy, it wasn't Jolly at all. Up until just now, I've always kept that to myself.

A slight pause.

Mebbe what I'm trying t'say is that I've done these things – yet I've criticized them in others. When your husband said I could come, I thought to myself: this is a new start, Eileen. Jolly was a great one for new starts. He would often say: let's put the past behind us. I was a girl in the shirt factory when we met. He washed his hands before opening a book did Jolly. It was his care for everything. It made me feel very stupid at times. I still wonder if I've underestimated myself?

A slight pause.

Mebbe what I'm trying to say is – if I hadn't underestimated myself, Jolly would never have underestimated his-self. I think that's what marriage is sometimes.

A telephone rings in the house.

MARGARET: I shan't be a moment.

MARGARET *stands.*

EILEEN: Could it be America ringing?

MARGARET: Yes, it could.

EILEEN: I'll cross my fingers for you.

MARGARET: Do, please. Do cross your fingers.

EILEEN *stands up.*

EILEEN (*showing her*): Look.

MARGARET: We don't receive many calls. This might well be him at last.

MARGARET *goes into the house.*

NIKOLAI *and* MATTY *enter along the muddy lane.* MATTY *is without his rucksack.*

NIKOLAI: Is that my father telephoning?

EILEEN: I think so. Isn't it exciting?

NIKOLAI: Yes. It will mean we shall have the White Crane at Oka.

NIKOLAI *and* MATTY *enter the garden.*

The telephone stops ringing.

I would like to ask you if you receive telephone calls from America, too?

MATTY: Erm, it depends if you know someone.

NIKOLAI: When you are there did you make friends with American children?

MATTY: Not really, Nikolai.

NIKOLAI: Was this forbidden by the leaders of your group?

MATTY: No, because I went with my mother. My mother was thinking of emigrating there, but she soon changed her mind.

NIKOLAI: Emigrating?

MATTY: Yes.

NIKOLAI: Like my own mother?

MATTY: That's right.

NIKOLAI: My mother loved the Soviet Union a great deal. I must go to her.

NIKOLAI *runs towards the door.* MARGARET *enters from the house. They very nearly collide.*

MARGARET: Be careful, Nikolai.

NIKOLAI *picks himself up.*

You heard the telephone ringing, didn't you?

NIKOLAI: Yes?

MARGARET: It wasn't Daddy, unfortunately

NIKOLAI (*pulling a face*): Oh.

MARGARET *puts her arm around* NIKOLAI*'s shoulders.*

MARGARET: It was from the police. I'd forgotten, I have to take you to register with them. I've said we'll go this evening.

NIKOLAI: Why have they been naughty already?

MARGARET: They haven't. It's something every visitor must do.

NIKOLAI *wriggles free of his mother's arm. He looks up at her.*

NIKOLAI: Mummy, Daddy will ring us from America, won't he?

MARGARET: I hope so.

NIKOLAI: I have told Matty he definitely will.

MARGARET: And I've told you it's not certain, haven't I?

NIKOLAI: Yes.

MARGARET: I'm sorry, Matty, it isn't certain.

MATTY: No.

MARGARET: And Nikolai knows that. (*Looking him in the eye.*) It's very stupid, isn't it, to go getting yourself built up.

NIKOLAI: Yes.

MARGARET: What happens when you do?

NIKOLAI: I find myself disappointed.

MARGARET: Exactly.

NIKOLAI: But, Mummy, he will ring, won't he?

MARGARET: Nikolai, because you want something, it doesn't mean it happens, does it?

NIKOLAI: No. But, Mummy, he will ring, won't he?

MARGARET: Of course he'll ring, pet.

NIKOLAI *looks at* EILEEN.

MARGARET (*to* EILEEN): He might not. (*To* NIKOLAI.) I know you want it so much.

MARGARET *puts her arm around NIKOLAI's shoulders.*

NIKOLAI: I thought it might be Daddy on the telephone.

MARGARET: It wasn't, was it?

NIKOLAI: No, it was the police for Matty.

MARGARET: Have you helped sort him out?

NIKOLAI (*brighter*): Yes.

MARGARET: Have you camped before, Matty?

MATTY: Erm – yes, I have. Well, rather, I've been youth hostelling once or twice.

MARGARET: That's what I used to do, to and from college, when I was a student. Did you enjoy it?

MATTY: Well, quite.

MARGARET: Not much?

MATTY: Not really.

MARGARET: It was a necessity for me. It was a way of travelling. I bicycled to and from college.

MATTY: Were you at university?

MARGARET: I was at teacher training in Cambridge.

NIKOLAI *wriggles free of his mother's arm.*

NIKOLAI: Mummy, what is youth hostelling?

MATTY (*going to him*): It's a lot of smelly feet, Nikolai.

EILEEN: No, it's not, don't confuse him.

MARGARET: It's a way of having a cheap holiday. People who like the countryside and who haven't a car, or who can't afford expensive train fares – they go youth hostelling. Don't they?

MATTY: Sometimes.

NIKOLAI: Is it like a hotel?

MATTY: Well, not really.

MARGARET: It's like a very cheap hotel, isn't it?

MATTY: Yes.

MARGARET: Everyone sleeps in a dormitory, and in the morning you help with the chores, like washing-up, and sweeping, and clearing the leaves in the garden. It's very popular with English people.

NIKOLAI: Were you organized by the leaders of your group?

MATTY: Well, I went with two friends.

NIKOLAI: Is it like my Young Pioneers?

MARGARET: It's similar in that people share a comradeship, yes.

NIKOLAI: I think I understand.

MARGARET: You don't actually, Nikolai.

NIKOLAI: I do, Mummy.

MARGARET *puts her arm around* NIKOLAI's *shoulders.*

MARGARET: He finds the concept of doing something on his own a very difficult one.

NIKOLAI (*looking up at her*): Why?

MARGARET: What did Matty just say?

NIKOLAI *wriggles free.*

NIKOLAI: Were your two friends children like me?

MATTY: Yes.

NIKOLAI: Did you elect a leader between you?

MATTY: No.

NIKOLAI: But what if there was a squabble?

MATTY: Well, there was, that was the problem. We bickered all the time.

NIKOLAI: We bicker, too, at my Young Pioneer Palace.

MATTY: What's that?

MARGARET: It's similar to the scouts. Every summer boys and girls go to a Young Pioneer camp. Don't you?

NIKOLAI: Yes. For our holiday together.

MARGARET: I know you all sleep in dormitories, but it isn't like a youth hostel. Matty went on his own.

NIKOLAI: Matty is a big boy?

MARGARET *puts her arm around* NIKOLAI's *shoulders.*

MARGARET: It's so hard to explain.

NIKOLAI: Yes, it is.

He wriggles free.

Mummy, Matty went on holiday on his own, didn't he?

NIKOLAI: Yes.

NIKOLAI: There were no leaders in his small group?

MARGARET: That's right.

NIKOLAI: Mummy, when will I be an independent boy like Matty?

MARGARET: You do understand, don't you?

NIKOLAI: Daddy has told me.

MARGARET: Has he?

NIKOLAI: Yes.

MARGARET: I wonder if Daddy shouldn't be more careful.

EILEEN: He's independent now, aren't you?

NIKOLAI: No.

MARGARET: I feel sure Matty would like a wash?

MATTY: I'm not very dirty.

MARGARET: Why don't you go and show him where the bathroom is.

NIKOLAI: Come with me, Matty.

NIKOLAI *and* MATTY *go into the house.*

EILEEN: His English is astonishing.

MARGARET: Yes, he has rather a rough ride at school. He's much better than his teacher, and she knows it. It has been quite a sticky problem, actually.

EILEEN: I can imagine.

MARGARET: He did make the mistake of correcting her. He's had to learn. He sits at his homework thinking of ways to say sentences badly.

EILEEN: Did you teach him from a baby?

MARGARET: No, not at all. He began at school with everyone else. It was Pavel who persuaded me it was churlish to sit back and pretend I couldn't help him. My children are inevitably a little different. Their friends are intrigued. Occasionally suspicious. Particularly their parents. I've tried to be quite quiet with Nikolai. I had the older children do French. It's difficult now because he thinks in English. He's streets ahead of the other children.

EILEEN: Are you worried?

MARGARET: No. Not quite. I think I may be though. Pavel pushes him a great deal.

EILEEN: At school?

MARGARET: At school and at home. I don't want to see him hurt, Eileen.

EILEEN: I know what yer mean. We were just the same with ours. I worried myself t'death sometimes. Needlessly. Yet children will be what they'll be, won't they? Despite our wishes. Our fears. I've come to the conclusion that all yer can be is as selfless as you can.

MARGARET *smiles.*

NIKOLAI *enters. He stops.*

MARGARET: You're not interrupting us. What is it?

NIKOLAI (*going to her*): Mummy, when Matty is finished, may I take him to see the Demoiselle Cranes?

MARGARET: Of course you may.

EILEEN: What are they?

NIKOLAI: It is a crane which is only a little like the Siberian.

MARGARET: They're in paddocks.

NIKOLAI: Yes, in enclosures. We can walk there.

EILEEN: Matty will like that.

NIKOLAI: Mummy, when we have seen the Demoiselle Cranes, may I take Matty swimming?

MARGARET: No, it's too cold.

NIKOLAI: I have my bathing costume.

MARGARET: I've said it's too cold, Nikolai.

NIKOLAI: Yes.

A slight pause.

May I then take him to see the White-naped Crane?

MARGARET: You can do that.

NIKOLAI: I would like to go on my bicycle.

MARGARET: Matty may borrow mine.

NIKOLAI: Mummy, may we call on Dmitri?

MARGARET: No.

NIKOLAI: He was thinking of going swimming this afternoon.

MARGARET: Nikolai, you won't be going anywhere if you carry on like this.

NIKOLAI: Yes.

MATTY *enters.*

MARGARET: I'm sorry, Matty, I don't want you messing about in the river. It still has ice in it.

MATTY: He said his friends will be there.

MARGARET: His friends can wait for a few days.

MATTY *joins them.*

I'd like you to settle in first.

MATTY: I don't mind.

MARGARET: We'll see about swimming later. What I may do is ask Nikolai to invite his friends here.

NIKOLAI: Dmitri wants to ask Matty something.

MARGARET: I bet he does. Dmitri's a ruffian. I don't like you playing with him.

NIKOLAI: He set fire to the red flags.

MARGARET: I know he did. He's lucky to be alive.

NIKOLAI: He's only alive because he is the policeman's son.

MARGARET: Not quite. Dmitri's eleven, Matty. He has a winning smile. You know that, don't you, Nikolai?

NIKOLAI: Yes.

MARGARET: When he gets you running about for him?

NIKOLAI: Yes.

NIKOLAI *shrugs.*

But I cannot help it. Little Dmitri is infectious.

MARGARET: He's heading for trouble. I don't want you playing with him while Matty's here. You're far too old for him.

NIKOLAI: Yes.

A slight pause.

Mummy, may I have all my other friends come and meet Matty?

MARGARET: Yes, you may. I'm only asking to know where you are.

NIKOLAI: Yes.

MARGARET: Be grown up.

NIKOLAI: Yes.

A slight pause.

We are going to see the Demoiselle, and the White-naped Cranes. Come with me, Matty.

MARGARET: Have a good time both of you.

NIKOLAI *and* MATTY *go.*

EILEEN *puts her coat on.*

Would you like to go inside?

EILEEN: No, I don't mind.

MARGARET: This is almost the first day of spring. It still gets very cold in the evening.

A slight pause.

EILEEN: Were you a teacher at home?

MARGARET: I taught with my father for a year. He was the headmaster of a tiny Quaker school in Tunbridge Wells.

EILEEN: D'you see anything of him?

MARGARET: No, nothing at all. In fact, both my parents died some years ago.

EILEEN *sits.*

When I married I became a Soviet citizen.

EILEEN: Did you miss England?

MARGARET: I still do, to some extent. It's gentility and refinement. It was obviously a big move to fall in love.

MARGARET *sits.*

I miss the silly things, like the run to Brighton in the car.

EILEEN: Have you taught over here?

MARGARET: Occasionally, yes. It still isn't easy to be completely accepted. Even now people will be suspicious from time to time. I'm Pavel's secretary, really. Oka's a large reserve, much of it wild and forested. At the moment thousands of acres are underwater with the melting ice.

EILEEN: It can't be easy.

MARGARET: No, but that's what makes it exciting. My husband has assistance from the foresters.

She smiles.

I was, and still am, a Marxist. Much to my father's chagrin.

EILEEN: Was he upset?

MARGARET: Oh, he thought me naive. We wrote regularly.

EILEEN: It's not the same though, is it?

MARGARET: No. It was very difficult for them. Especially when we began a family.

EILEEN: Was it difficult for you?

MARGARET: Yes, it was quite. It's taken a long time to remove those suspicions. I was on my own with Edvard. Everywhere I went people hid their gaze. But children are children. His going to kindergarten helped a great deal.

She smiles.

I miss the teas on the lawn, and lemonade. I even miss the school with the children playing cricket. My father was a lifelong pacifist.

EILEEN: Was he?

MARGARET: My whole family were.

EILEEN: Jolly believed in pacifism. He used to say that wars were only a temporary solution.

MARGARET *smiles.*

MARGARET: We sent photographs of the children. He was a brave man. In many ways Pavel is not unlike him. My grandfather was shot in the Great War, by a firing squad, for refusing to fight.

EILEEN: There's so much violence about, isn't there?

MARGARET: He'd said he could never kill. It helped me think about justice.

EILEEN: I argued with Jolly. I wasn't sure.

MARGARET: I first came here as a student. To a youth festival in Moscow. When I first met Pavel he wanted to know about rock-'n'-roll and Teddy-boys. I was almost the last person to ask. I saw these young men with cardboard guitars, and one record, which they mimed to unceasingly.

EILEEN: You weren't a rock-'n'-roller?

MARGARET: I was playing with an orchestra.

EILEEN: D'you still?

MARGARET: Only periodically. We've tried to interest Nikolai, but he isn't keen. I don't believe you should force children. He much prefers the outdoors.

EILEEN *fastens her coat.*

Why don't I take you in?

EILEEN: In a minute. I'm quite happy.

MARGARET: My grandfather was a good musician. I'm told he was.

EILEEN: It's awful what people will do to each other, isn't it?

MARGARET: Yes.

EILEEN: Did you come back to meet your husband?

MARGARET: We weren't married then. I was eager to see Moscow for myself, if I could, away from the group. By then I'd finished college and was busily teaching.

She picks up the sock from the workbasket and puts it on her lap.

I never meant to stay. I didn't even bring my cello. At the bottom of my bag I had Jerry Lee Lewis, and Little Richard. Rafiya still plays them.

EILEEN: Were they Pavel's favourites?

MARGARET: I can't really remember, Eileen. I think so, yes. Like most young people we were growing up.

She begins to darn the sock.

In fact, in a funny way, I think it was my father who knew I was coming here forever. He kept asking why I wasn't taking the cello.

EILEEN: What did your grandfather play?

MARGARET: The piano. There is a natural way of things; a course of justice which is right for one person and not another.

EILEEN: Your grandfather was brave.

MARGARET: Very, I think. Pavel was, too. And his sister. We met at his sister's flat. It was difficult then to meet a Russian, in a Russian home.

MARGARET *smiles.*

EILEEN: Can I help you?

MARGARET: No, don't be silly.

EILEEN: It's years since I darned.

MARGARET: Is it:

EILEEN: My goodness I used to.

MARGARET: I wouldn't miss darning.

EILEEN: You didn't see your father again?

MARGARET: No, unfortunately.

EILEEN: There is a price for whatever we do, isn't there?

MARGARET: Yes, I think there is, very much so.

EILEEN: If we're not careful criticism comes very cheap.

MARGARET *smiles.*

I wish Jolly was here.

MARGARET: Do you?

EILEEN: Yes, I do.

MARGARET: I wasn't at all sure about your coming.

EILEEN: Weren't you? You shouldn't worry about us.

MARGARET: I don't worry. Well, I do. I worry about Nikolai. I'm sure unnecessarily.

EILEEN *smiles.*

MARGARET *has finished darning. She snaps the wool between her fingers. She puts the wool and the needle in her workbasket. She takes a shirt from the bottom.*

EILEEN: You won't worry about us, will you?

MARGARET: No.

EILEEN: I know what you mean when you say there's a natural course of justice.

MARGARET: Do you?

EILEEN: Yes.

MARGARET: I wasn't doubting you.

EILEEN: I know you weren't.

MARGARET *smiles.*

MARGARET: The pinnacle of our life here is Pavel's work with the cranes.

EILEEN *holds up her crossed fingers.*

He's fought so tirelessly, and unselfishly. It has to work for him.

EILEEN: It will. Have you buttons to sew?

MARGARET: Yes.

EILEEN: Give it me.

EILEEN *takes the shirt.*

MARGARET: Why don't I take you in?

EILEEN: In a minute. Unless you want to?

MARGARET: No.

MARGARET *takes another shirt from the workbasket.*

EILEEN: I'm a dab hand at this.

MARGARET: We shouldn't be so long. I haven't even offered you tea.

The two women prepare to sew.

Scene Two

That night.

Pavel's small, wooden office which has a log-burning stove in one corner. Below the window is a desk, one side of which is crammed with files and papers. On the other side is an electric incubator. The desk also has a writing lamp, a telephone, and a swivel chair. Elsewhere is a bookcase untidily stuffed with periodicals and books.

The curtains are drawn. There are two campbeds, made up for the night, on the wooden floor. The writing lamp is on.

NIKOLAI *and* MATTY. NIKOLAI *is wearing trousers, a jumper, and his red scarf.*

NIKOLAI: This is the scarf of the Young Pioneers. Do you have a scarf, Matty?

MATTY: No.

NIKOLAI: When I am older I shall join the Komsomol, which is the Communist Union of Youth. At your school, what do they do when you are naughty?

MATTY: Erm – we get lines and extra prep.

NIKOLAI: What is prep?

MATTY: Extra homework.

NIKOLAI: And lines?

MATTY: Lines are completely ridiculous, Nikolai. Absolutely bloody pointless. They're given to demean us.

NIKOLAI: Why?

MATTY: A good question. We have to write out hundreds of times what we've done wrong.

NIKOLAI: When you are naughty?

MATTY: Yes.

NIKOLAI: Please may I ask you – are you often naughty at your school?

MATTY: Well – sometimes. It isn't quite like that though, not in the sixth form.

NIKOLAI: At my school they take away our scarfs. You will not inform my mother?

MATTY: No.

NIKOLAI: My scarf keeps on disappearing for being naughty.

There is a knock on the wooden door.

NIKOLAI *and* MATTY *look towards it.*

(*Quietly.*) Oh dear, oh dear. We must hide. Quickly. We must get under the covers.

NIKOLAI *and* MATTY *jump into their beds. They pull the blankets up to their necks.*

MATTY (*quietly*): Who is it?

The door opens.

MARGARET *enters.*

MARGARET: Are you both comfortable?

MATTY: Yes.

NIKOLAI: Yes, thank you, Mummy.

MARGARET: Have you plenty of logs?

NIKOLAI: Yes, Matty helped me to carry some.

MARGARET: Good. I've some news for you. Daddy's here.

NIKOLAI: Daddy is here?

NIKOLAI *jumps out of bed.*

MARGARET: Nikolai Pavlovich, why aren't you in your pyjamas?

NIKOLAI: Mummy, we, er –

A slight pause.

MARGARET: What did I say, Nikolai?

NIKOLAI: Yes.

MATTY *gets out of bed.*

MATTY: It's my fault.

MARGARET: Why aren't you in your pyjamas, Matty?

NIKOLAI: We were searching for his pyjamas. They've run away somewhere.

MARGARET: Don't be silly.

NIKOLAI: Yes, Mummy, they have. Gone. (*Looking at him.*) Where to, Matty?

MARGARET *looks at* MATTY.

MATTY: We were only talking.

MARGARET: Matty's more sense, hasn't he? I sometimes think you've not got the brains you were born with, Nikolai.

NIKOLAI: Pardon?

MARGARET: As it happens, it doesn't matter. I came to tell you to get dressed. Now, listen to me, Daddy's very tired. He's had a long journey from America.

NIKOLAI: But, Mummy, he has not telephoned us?

MARGARET: I know. He's tried, and couldn't get through.

NIKOLAI (*disappointed*): He has no eggs for us.

MARGARET *puts her arm around* NIKOLAI'*s shoulders.*

MARGARET: Look at me, Nikolai.

NIKOLAI *looks up at her.*

NIKOLAI: Please, Mummy?

MARGARET: He's three eggs. One has unfortunately died on the journey.

NIKOLAI: Three eggs?

MARGARET: Yes. Two are still alive.

NIKOLAI: Two eggs. We shall have the White Crane at Oka?

MARGARET: Yes.

NIKOLAI: I must go and find my Daddy, mustn't I?

MARGARET: No, he's coming here.

NIKOLAI: But my Daddy needs me.

PAVEL *enters. He is carrying a large portable incubator.*

NIKOLAI *rushes towards him.*

PAVEL: Careful.

EILEEN *follows* PAVEL *in.*

PAVEL *puts his arm around* NIKOLAI'*s shoulders.*

You were dressed quickly.

NIKOLAI: We were not undressed, Daddy.

PAVEL: Hello.

MATTY (*suddenly shyly*): Hello.

PAVEL: What do you think of our country?

MATTY: It's great.

PAVEL (*to* NIKOLAI): You two have made good friends?

NIKOLAI: Yes.

PAVEL (*to* MATTY): All boys must talk, I think. It is very good you talk. (*To* NIKOLAI.) When I am a student we stay awake all those nights.

NIKOLAI: Did you?

PAVEL: Of course. I was a little older than you, but – well, what does it matter?

MARGARET: Pavel.

PAVEL: Yes, your Mummy is right as usual. I am very tired. I have come a long way today.

NIKOLAI: Please, Daddy, please may I see the eggs?

PAVEL: Of course.

NIKOLAI: Thank you.

MATTY: May I, please?

PAVEL: Of course. Both of you.

PAVEL *puts the incubator on the floor.*

I must remind you to be very, very careful. These are very precious.

NIKOLAI: Me first.

NIKOLAI *kneels by the incubator.*

MARGARET: Nikolai.

NIKOLAI: What, Mummy?

MARGARET: Don't overstep the mark.

NIKOLAI: No.

MATTY *kneels by the incubator.*

MATTY: What's happened to the one which has died?

PAVEL *kneels.*

PAVEL: I do not know yet. I will have to look into it. Tomorrow.

NIKOLAI: Me first.

MARGARET: Nikolai Pavlovich.

NIKOLAI (*looking up at her, shamefaced*): What?

MARGARET: Stand up.

NIKOLAI *stands up.*

EILEEN: He's only excited.

MARGARET: One more word out of you and a rocket will go up. Is that absolutely clear?

NIKOLAI: Yes.

A slight pause.

May I kneel again?

MARGARET: Yes.

NIKOLAI *kneels.*

PAVEL (*to* NIKOLAI): Has the electricity been put into the incubator?

NIKOLAI *looks at his mother.*

MARGARET: Nikolai's had it plugged in since the day you left.

PAVEL: I do not want them to get cold, you understand. This is what I have striven for, for ten years.

PAVEL *lifts the hinged lid of the incubator, revealed in a compartment at the top are three crane eggs.*

They look at them.

MATTY: Which is the dead one?

PAVEL: This one.

MATTY: Can I lift it out?

PAVEL: Yes.

MATTY *lifts it out.*

MATTY (*to* EILEEN): It's heavier than the ones Jolly had.

PAVEL: It has a chick inside it. Unfortunately, you know sometimes there is a weakness.

MATTY: It's still warm.

PAVEL: It is in the incubator – so, yes.

MATTY *puts the egg back.*

MATTY: These are the live ones?

PAVEL: Be very careful, please.

MATTY *lifts up a live egg.*

Only for a very short moment. You like?

MATTY: Yes.

PAVEL: Inside is a little Siberian Crane chick for Oka. Please put him down now.

MATTY *returns the egg to the incubator.*

You would like to listen to him?

MATTY: Yes.

PAVEL: You will hear he is alive in there.

PAVEL *takes a stethoscope from the pocket of his suit jacket.*

MATTY *puts the stethoscope on. He listens.*

You hear him?

MATTY: Eh, you can, it's absolutely brilliant.

PAVEL: He is moving about in there, just a little bit.

MATTY *continues to listen.*

EILEEN: Matty, give Nikolai a go.

MATTY: In a minute. I haven't finished yet.

PAVEL: Just for one more moment, and then for my son.

A pause.

EILEEN: Matty.

MATTY: What are they doing when they're moving about?

PAVEL: It is important they do not settle, you know.

NIKOLAI: Daddy, in the wild the mother bird turns the egg, doesn't she?

PAVEL: Of course. We must turn the eggs, too. Every two hours we must do that.

NIKOLAI: Daddy, the embryo is delicate, isn't it?

PAVEL: Until the nest of the Grey Crane we must be his mother. You are right, Nikolai. Until the cuckoo.

He taps MATTY *on the shoulder.*

I think for my son now, please.

MATTY *looks up. He takes the stethoscope off and gives it to* NIKOLAI.

NIKOLAI *stands up.*

NIKOLAI: Would you like to listen?

EILEEN: No, no, no, it's your turn.

NIKOLAI *kneels. He puts the stethoscope on and listens to the eggs.*

MARGARET *comes up behind him and leans over.*

MARGARET: Can you hear them?

NIKOLAI: Yes. It is like a little rustling.

MARGARET: Nikolai's heard them before, Matty.

NIKOLAI: Not the Siberian egg.

MARGARET: No, but similar. The Demoiselle Crane, and the White-naped Crane. (*Looking at him.*) Bed, Pavel.

PAVEL: We must put the eggs into the incubator now.

NIKOLAI: May I?

PAVEL: Yes.

NIKOLAI *stands up. He opens the lid of the other incubator. He transfers one of the live eggs.*

NIKOLAI: I should turn the egg over, too?

PAVEL: Yes.

NIKOLAI *turns the egg.*

MARGARET: They're not going to get any sleep, are they?

PAVEL: Not tonight. They must do this.

NIKOLAI *transfers the other live egg.*

MARGARET: I wonder if I shouldn't stay here?

PAVEL: They will be fine.

MARGARET: Why don't we take the incubator to our room?

PAVEL: It will be in the way. It is easier for them.

NIKOLAI *turns the egg.*

MATTY *stands. He picks up the remaining egg. He gives it to* NIKOLAI.

NIKOLAI *looks at* PAVEL.

In there, yes, until the morning.

NIKOLAI *puts the egg into the incubator. He closes the lid.*

EILEEN *goes to* MATTY.

EILEEN (*quietly*): No fooling about.

MATTY: No.

EILEEN: You know what a responsibility this is, don't you?

MATTY: Yes.

MARGARET: Do you, Matty?

MATTY: Look – I'm not a child.

NIKOLAI *goes to* PAVEL.

NIKOLAI: Daddy, the incubator must stay at ninety-eight degrees?

PAVEL: Yes.

MARGARET: I'll come down at three o'clock and check you're both all right.

PAVEL: No, it is not necessary.

MARGARET: I'm coming down at three o'clock, Pavel.

PAVEL: No. There is the telephone. If there is a problem they will pick it up and they will ring. My son will do this.

MARGARET: Are you sure?

PAVEL: Of course.

MARGARET *smiles and goes to* PAVEL.

MARGARET: I hope you're right.

PAVEL: I am.

MARGARET: I'll take Eileen back. Don't be long, will you?

PAVEL: I will be one moment only.

MARGARET *goes to* EILEEN.

EILEEN: Good night.

MARGARET *and* EILEEN *go.*

PAVEL *takes a small box from his pocket.*

PAVEL: I have this for you.

NIKOLAI *takes it.*

NIKOLAI: What is it?

PAVEL: Open it and see.

NIKOLAI *opens the box.*

It is a very small pocket calculator. No batteries, no problems. It works by the sun.

NIKOLAI *is madly tapping on the keys.*

MATTY: It's a solar calculator.

NIKOLAI: You have one?

MATTY: Yes.

NIKOLAI: I have one, too, now.

NIKOLAI *trys to undo it.*

MATTY: What're you doing?

NIKOLAI: I'm trying to take it apart to see how it works, Matty.

PAVEL: I will tell you in the morning.

MATTY: It doesn't come apart like that.

NIKOLAI: Why?

MATTY: It just doesn't, that's all.

NIKOLAI: Well, it should.

MATTY: You'll break it.

NIKOLAI *stops.*

NIKOLAI: Daddy, how does it work from the sun?

PAVEL *ruffles* NIKOLAI's *hair.*

PAVEL: It has a photo-electric cell. You are a jack-in-the-box tonight. Too many questions. I will explain it all in the morning. I must go.

PAVEL *goes. The door closes behind him.*

MATTY: I can tell you how it works, Nikolai.

Scene Three

The office. A bright, spring morning, two days later.

The curtains are drawn and the door is open. On each of the campbeds is an anorak and a rucksack.

PAVEL, NIKOLAI, MATTY, MARGARET *and* EILEEN. NIKOLAI *is wearing wellingtons, and* MATTY *has walking boots.*

PAVEL *is by the electric incubator. He opens it and very carefully he transfers one of the live eggs to a small portable incubator.*

The others watch.

PAVEL *transfers the second egg. He closes and fastens the lid of the portable incubator. He turns the electric incubator off at the plug.*

NIKOLAI *and* MATTY *go to their anoraks. They put them on.* NIKOLAI's *anorak is not as bright, and is a much poorer quality than* MATTY's.

MARGARET *goes to* NIKOLAI. *She helps him. She does up the zip at the front.*

MATTY *does his own zip.* EILEEN *watches.*

NIKOLAI *and* MATTY *put their rucksacks on their backs. They jiggle up and down to get them comfortable.*

The others watch.

PAVEL *goes to* NIKOLAI *and ruffles his hair.* NIKOLAI *beams.*

MATTY *smiles at* EILEEN. EILEEN *smiles, and then looks down for a second.*

NIKOLAI *goes to the portable incubator and picks it up by the handle.*

PAVEL *watches.*

MATTY *joins* NIKOLAI. *They go out through the door.*

A slight pause.

MARGARET *turns to* PAVEL.

MARGARET: It's such a long way.

PAVEL: Sometimes, I think, we must journey for ourselves.

He turns to EILEEN.

Jolly, he would have given the eggs to the boys, dear lady?

EILEEN: Yes, he would.

MARGARET *goes to* PAVEL. *She runs her hand across his stomach.* PAVEL *puts his arm around her.* MARGARET *kisses him once on the lips.*

The three adults are still.

Scene Four

Later that morning.

The vast Oka forest which is submerged in water and melting snow. The hundreds of silver birch trees still have no leaves, and they look almost barren as they twist and turn from the flood water towards the sky.

A cold, spring sunlight.

There is a tiny island which the flooding has left. The grass is rough and dead. A silver birch is growing.

On the flood water is a boat with an outboard motor. The propeller is raised and has grass and twigs around it.

NIKOLAI *and* MATTY *are in the boat.* MATTY *is sitting in the bows.* NIKOLAI *is at the stern clearing the propeller.*

NIKOLAI: It is another twenty kilometers to the Grey Crane's nest.

MATTY: Let me have a look.

He joins NIKOLAI *at the stern.*

NIKOLAI: I can do it, thank you, Matty.

MATTY: You can't do everything. There's some things I'm better at than you. I know about boats.

MATTY *leans out, beside* NIKOLAI, *towards the propeller.*

NIKOLAI: Please, you are pushing me away.

MATTY: It's you, you're absolutely, pathetically, useless.

NIKOLAI: Pardon?

MATTY: If only you'd budge I'd have the space.

NIKOLAI *moves.*

NIKOLAI: Matty, we should stop now.

MATTY: My brilliance is saving the day here, Nikolai.

NIKOLAI: The water is too shallow.

MATTY: It's best if we go as far as we can in the boat. Don't you agree?

NIKOLAI *shrugs*.

NIKOLAI: I have tried to tell you my thoughts.

MATTY: Doesn't it get deeper farther on?

NIKOLAI: No, Matty, it doesn't. We are off the river now.

MATTY: Nurd, why didn't you say?

NIKOLAI: Pardon? What is a nurd?

MATTY: Nothing. It's an expression of endearment.

NIKOLAI: Matty, nurd, sometimes your ears are blind to what I have to say.

MATTY: You sound just like your mother.

NIKOLAI: Mummy. Why?

MATTY: She's a nurd if ever there was one.

NIKOLAI *smiles*.

NIKOLAI: You like my mother? I love her, too.

NIKOLAI *steps out of the boat into the shallow flood water.*

Please may I ask you – I would like to ask if all mothers are as strict in England?

MATTY *leaves the propeller and sits in the boat.*

MATTY: Well, not really. It depends. Some are.

NIKOLAI: Is yours, Matty?

MATTY: No.

NIKOLAI *picks up the incubator and carries it towards the island.*

NIKOLAI: My friends at school, their mothers are not as strict as mine.

MATTY: You know what I think?

NIKOLAI: No?

MATTY: Well, you have to educate your parents.

NIKOLAI: Pardon?

MATTY: Put your foot down now and again.

NIKOLAI *puts the incubator down. He looks nonplussed. He walks back towards the boat.*

NIKOLAI: Oh, I could never do that. It is wrong to insult our parents.

MATTY: You'll have to eventually.

NIKOLAI: Why?

MATTY: If you want to grow up.

NIKOLAI: Pardon, no, Matty. My parents have great respect for me.

MATTY: It doesn't get you very far though, does it?

NIKOLAI: I do not like you insulting my mother. Nurd is not a nice word. You are a nurd.

NIKOLAI *picks up a rucksack and carries it towards the island.*

MATTY: Don't get upset.

NIKOLAI: I am not upset. I do not like you when you think you are wonderful.

MATTY: I do, do I?

NIKOLAI: Yes, you do.

MATTY: That's because I am, Nikolai.

NIKOLAI *puts the rucksack down.*

NIKOLAI: No, you are a little boy like me.

He walks back to the boat.

Please, we have to shake hands now.

He offers his hand. MATTY *hesitates.*

We must if I am to be your friend again.

The two boys shake hands.

NIKOLAI *pushes the boat, through the flood water, to the island.*

MATTY *steps out of the boat.*

Please, would you fasten the rope to the tree.

MATTY: I'm not a dogsbody, Nikolai.

NIKOLAI: Pardon?

MATTY: I'm not your slave.

A slight pause.

NIKOLAI *takes the painter from the bows of the boat.* MATTY *pushes him away.*

Get off, I'm doing it.

MATTY *takes the painter and fastens it to the tree.*

NIKOLAI *takes the rucksack from the boat and puts it with the other one and the incubator.*

The two boys look at one another. NIKOLAI *walks to* MATTY *and offers his hand.*

What's the point of that if it makes no difference?

NIKOLAI: In my country this is the way children say we are sorry to one another.

MATTY: Yes, well, I'm not sorry, and I'm not a child.

NIKOLAI: When we shake hands we must honour what we have done.

MATTY: Yes, well you can fuck off.

NIKOLAI: Pardon?

MATTY: Leave me alone. Okay?

NIKOLAI: Yes.

NIKOLAI *walks to the rucksacks and the incubator.*

The two boys are silent for a moment.

NIKOLAI *walks to* MATTY *offering his hand.*

Please, Matty, this is very wrong.

MATTY: What did I just say?

NIKOLAI: Yes.

NIKOLAI *walks back to the rucksacks and the incubator.*

The two boys are silent for a moment.

MATTY: I'm in charge. Okay?

NIKOLAI: Yes.

MATTY *walks to the incubator and kneels down. He opens the lid.*

NIKOLAI *kneels.*

Are you going to turn them, Matty?

MATTY *looks at his watch.*

MATTY: It's an hour and fifty minutes since we did them last.

MATTY *turns both the eggs. He closes the lid and stands up. He begins to put his rucksack on.*

A slight pause.

NIKOLAI *stands up.*

NIKOLAI: Excuse me, but you did not check the temperature.

MATTY: Well done, Nikolai.

MATTY *has his rucksack on. He kneels by the incubator and opens the lid.*

It's ninety-seven degrees. That's within the limits, isn't it.

NIKOLAI *kneels.*

NIKOLAI: No, Matty, it isn't.

NIKOLAI *leans over.* MATTY *covers the thermometer with his hands.*

MATTY: Stop trying to look, I've read it correctly.

NIKOLAI *trys to move* MATTY's *hands.*

NIKOLAI: I must check, too, please.

MATTY *pushes* NIKOLAI *away.* NIKOLAI *falls onto his back.* MATTY *closes the incubator and stands up. He picks the incubator up by the handle.*

NIKOLAI *stands up.*

I am not going on with you. You are a spoilt baby.

MATTY: Well, you'll have to.

NIKOLAI: No, not until we shake hands.

MATTY: The eggs will die then, won't they?

Silence.

NIKOLAI: Please – please may I ask you to tell me what I have done wrong?

MATTY: Wrong?

NIKOLAI: Yes.

A pause.

There were no leaders in your small group, Matty.

A slight pause.

I think you are a very unkind boy.

MATTY *walks to the boat.*

MATTY: I'm going back the way we came.

NIKOLAI: No, you will not find it on your own.

MATTY: Well, if you show me, Nikolai?

NIKOLAI: I would have to see my father.

A slight pause.

Please, Matty, you must raise the temperature in the incubator.

A slight pause.

MATTY: Is it dangerously low?

NIKOLAI: Yes, it is.

A slight pause.

Please, Matty, you must be as quick as you can.

A slight pause.

Please – please may I ask you why you want the eggs to die?

A slight pause.

May I show you?

A slight pause.

MATTY *walks to* NIKOLAI *and puts the incubator down.* NIKOLAI *kneels and begins to undo the rucksack at his feet.* MATTY *takes his rucksack off and puts it down.* NIKOLAI *stands up.*

You must find the pan and the gas-ring from the bottom of my rucksack.

MATTY *kneels. He takes a portable gas-ring and a pan from* NIKOLAI's *rucksack.*

You must take the hot-water bottle too now.

MATTY *takes a rubber hot water-bottle from the rucksack. He looks up at* NIKOLAI.

Please empty the water into the pan.

MATTY *unscrews the top of the hot-water bottle. He empties a small amount of water into the pan.* NIKOLAI *bends down and delves into his rucksack for matches. He gives them to* MATTY. MATTY *lights the gas. He puts the pan on.*

A slight pause.

NIKOLAI *kneels.*

A pause.

MATTY: Nikolai.

MATTY *offers his hand.*

A slight pause.

NIKOLAI *shakes his head.*

Why not?

NIKOLAI: Now we must wait for the water to be hot.

MATTY *picks up the hot-water bottle and offers it to* NIKOLAI.

MATTY: Would you like to do it?

NIKOLAI *takes the hot-water bottle. He delves into his rucksack and takes out a Sony Walkman complete with headphones.*

NIKOLAI: Do you have one of these, Matty?

MATTY *undoes his rucksack. He takes out his Sony Walkman.*

MATTY: Yours is better than mine, it's the older version.

NIKOLAI: Better?

MATTY: I had one, but I sold it.

NIKOLAI: Daddy brought me mine from America. All my friends at school they love to put the headphones on, and hear the popular tapes.

NIKOLAI *puts the headphones on.*

We have a problem with batteries in our family.

NIKOLAI *presses the buttons on the cassette recorder.*

Look, it does not work.

He dances on his knees as if there was music playing.

MATTY *opens his cassette-recorder and takes out the batteries.*

MATTY: Well, would you like mine?

NIKOLAI *stops dancing and takes the headphones off. He hesitates.*

I'd like you to have them.

NIKOLAI *takes the calculator from a pocket in his anorak. He looks at it for a moment.*

NIKOLAI: Would you accept this?

MATTY: They're a present, Nikolai.

NIKOLAI: Oh, dear.

MATTY: What's the matter?

NIKOLAI: I must give you something in return.

MATTY: I don't want anything.

NIKOLAI: Oh dear.

MATTY: They're yours.

NIKOLAI: No, I could not do that.

NIKOLAI *stands up. He looks at the pan.*

May I do this please, Matty?

MATTY: Yes.

NIKOLAI *puts his calculator away. He turns the gas-ring off and begins to fill the hot-water bottle from the pan.*

MATTY *takes NIKOLAI's Walkman and puts his batteries into it.*

NIKOLAI: What are you doing?

MATTY: I'm giving you them.

NIKOLAI: No, you must not.

MATTY: Well, I am. There.

MATTY *puts NIKOLAI's Walkman back.*

NIKOLAI *puts the pan down and screws the top on the hot-water bottle.*

NIKOLAI: Now you must take the cold hot-water bottle from the incubator.

MATTY *opens the small compartment at the bottom. He slides out another rubber hot-water bottle. NIKOLAI gives MATTY the hot one, MATTY gives NIKOLAI the cold one. MATTY looks up at NIKOLAI.*

That's right, back in there.

MATTY *slides the fresh hot water bottle into the compartment at the bottom of the incubator and closes it.*

NIKOLAI *kneels down.*

Matty, you must wait and see if this works now.

MATTY *offers his hand.*

NIKOLAI *delves into an anorak pocket and finds a small badge.*

Would you accept this? It is not much. It is a small badge of Vladimir Lenin, which I have for swopping at school.

MATTY: Yes.

MATTY *takes it. He pins it to his anorak.*

NIKOLAI: You are like a Russian boy now.

MATTY *offers his hand.*

Matty, I will not shake your hand until you tell me what I have done wrong?

A slight pause.

MATTY: Well, that's particularly difficult.

NIKOLAI: Why?

MATTY: Nikolai, please, just shake my hand.

A slight pause.

You're hurting me.

NIKOLAI: Why?

MATTY: You're hurting me, Nikolai.

NIKOLAI: Please, Matty, tell me why I'm hurting you?

A slight pause.

MATTY: It's particularly difficult because you haven't done anything wrong.

A slight pause.

NIKOLAI: I don't understand. Matty, I must know.

MATTY: It's not you, you idiot. It's me.

NIKOLAI: Pardon?

MATTY: It's me.

A slight pause.

NIKOLAI: Pardon?

MATTY *offers his hand.*

MATTY: Look, just shake my hand before I die or something.

NIKOLAI: You will not die.

MATTY: Oh, for fuck's sake.

NIKOLAI: What is a fucks?

MATTY: Shake it, you bastard.

NIKOLAI: What is a bastard?

MATTY: Shake it. Please.

NIKOLAI *shakes his hand.*

Thank you.

Silence.

NIKOLAI: May I ask – what is a fucks and what is a bastards?

MATTY: They're swear-words. They're nothing.

NIKOLAI: Like nurd?

MATTY: No, stronger than nurd.

MATTY *stands up. He picks up the incubator and carries it away a few feet. He puts it down and kneels.*

NIKOLAI *stands up.*

NIKOLAI: May I ask you why you don't like my mother?

MATTY: I do. She's great.

MATTY *opens the incubator.*

NIKOLAI: You know, Matty, sometimes you are a boy who always wants his own way.

NIKOLAI *kneels. He packs up and fastens both the rucksacks.*

MATTY *closes the incubator.*

NIKOLAI *stands up and gives* MATTY *his rucksack.*

MATTY *stands up.*

Please, what was the temperature?

MATTY: Ninety-eight-and-a-half degrees. That's right, isn't it?

NIKOLAI: Yes, it is.

MATTY *puts his rucksack on.* NIKOLAI *puts his on.* MATTY *picks up the incubator by the handle.*

NIKOLAI *walks past* MATTY *and continues on the journey.* MATTY *follows him.*

Scene Five

Later.

The dense silver birches of the Oka forest. A large island which the flooding has left. The grass is thick and coarse, and wild with bulrushes. On the ground, between the trees, is a Grey Crane's nest made of twigs and brown grass.

A cold, evening sunlight.

NIKOLAI *enters. He looks towards the nest.*

MATTY *enters. He stops. He puts the incubator down and sits on it.*

NIKOLAI: Please do not sit on the incubator.

MATTY *stands up.*

NIKOLAI *runs up the slight incline towards the nest, and kneels down beside it.*

MATTY: Is that it?

NIKOLAI *picks up a Grey Crane egg from the nest.*

NIKOLAI: We are here at last, Matty.

MATTY *runs up the incline to the nest. He kneels.*

MATTY: We've found it.

NIKOLAI: Yes.

MATTY *picks up an egg.*

MATTY: Where's the mother?

NIKOLAI: Our footsteps will have frightened her away.

NIKOLAI *puts the Grey Crane egg back in the nest.*

Matty, we must not go on like this, you and me.

MATTY *puts his egg back into the nest.*

Are you tired?

MATTY: Yes.

NIKOLAI: I am exhausted by tiredness.

MATTY: Are you feeling all right?

NIKOLAI: No, Matty, I am not. I am finding it all so very hard, my English and everything, and you.

MATTY *looks down.*

This is not right between us.

MATTY *looks up.*

MATTY: I'm sorry, Nikolai.

NIKOLAI *stands up.*

NIKOLAI: You must be the cuckoo now.

NIKOLAI *walks to the incubator and carries it back to the nest. He puts it down and kneels.*

Please may I ask you – well, I would like to know if you are the same with your other friends?

MATTY *takes his wristwatch off. He offers it to* NIKOLAI.

NIKOLAI *shows the wristwatch on his own arm.*

I do not need it, you know.

MATTY: Well, if I have anything, it's yours.

MATTY *puts his wristwatch back on his arm.*

NIKOLAI: There is one thing. Please may I ask – well, I would like to ask if you will speak to my mother for me?

MATTY: Yes.

NIKOLAI: Matty, please may I visit you at your home near Middlesborough?

MATTY: Well, of course you may, you idiot.

NIKOLAI: If I ask my mother she will only say 'no'. If you ask her, then I will chip in and be enthusiastic.

MATTY: Yes.

NIKOLAI: I would love to meet your friends and see them for myself.

A slight pause.

MATTY: Well, do you imagine they're all as bad as me?

NIKOLAI: Is Britain a very different country from the Soviet Union?

A slight pause.

MATTY: Yes, I think so.

NIKOLAI: You are very lucky to come here.

A slight pause.

MATTY: I know you don't like me, Nikolai.

NIKOLAI: I think you are a boy who always feels sorry for himself, Matty.

MATTY (*gently*): Do I?

NIKOLAI: Yes, you do.

A slight pause.

MATTY: Do I seem self-pitying?

NIKOLAI: Yes.

A slight pause.

Matty, we must be the cuckoo.

NIKOLAI *opens the incubator.*

You must pass me the eggs from the Grey Crane nest.

MATTY *picks up a Grey Crane egg and gives it to* NIKOLAI. NIKOLAI *puts it in the incubator.*

The mother will not be far away, we must be very quick.

MATTY *quickly picks up two more eggs from the Grey Crane's nest.*

Without being slapdash, Matty.

MATTY *slows down. He gives them to* NIKOLAI. NIKOLAI *puts them into the incubator.*

Now you must find the artificial egg from your rucksack.

MATTY *takes off his rucksack. He opens it and finds the pot egg. He gives it to* NIKOLAI. NIKOLAI *puts it in the nest.*

Now, please, you must pass me, very carefully, the fertile eggs of the White Siberian Crane.

MATTY *carefully picks up one of the Siberian Crane eggs. He holds it in his left hand.*

A slight pause.

He offers his right hand to NIKOLAI.

A slight pause.

MATTY: Why not?

NIKOLAI: Matty, I have let you do everything, haven't I?

MATTY: Please, Nikolai.

NIKOLAI *stands up. He moves away. He stops.*

NIKOLAI: I will come over here, if that is what you want?

A slight pause.

Look, I am over here.

A slight pause.

They will get cold and the mother will never come back.

A slight pause.

Look, Matty.

MATTY *stands up. He offers his hand.*

MATTY: Why not, Nikolai?

NIKOLAI *hesitates.*

Please.

NIKOLAI: We should go home now, I think.

MATTY *has the egg in his hand.*

Matty, what else can I do?

MATTY: Just shake my hand.

A slight pause.

NIKOLAI *shakes his head.*

NIKOLAI: No, you are a very naughty boy.

MATTY *picks up the second Siberian Crane egg from the incubator. He presses his fingers around them.*

MATTY: I'll break them.

NIKOLAI: No, Matty, you would not do that.

MATTY: I would.

NIKOLAI: Matty, you are a nice boy really.

MATTY *hits the two eggs together. The shells crack. The eggs break. The embryos come out into his hands.*

Silence.

Look what you have gone and done.

Silence.

You have gone and killed those eggs. How could you go and do that? I hate you.

Silence.

I hate you, I hate you, I hate you. I will kick you if you do not give those eggs to me.

NIKOLAI *goes to* MATTY. *He cups his hands.* MATTY *gives him the broken shells and the embryos.*

I will kick you if you do not get out of my sight.

MATTY *moves away from the nest.*

If you come near me again I will kick you, and kick you, and kick you.

NIKOLAI *kneels.*

I wish you would get out of my sight I hate you so much.

MATTY *moves away a few more feet.*

NIKOLAI *is looking at the embryos.*

Silence.

MATTY: Is it possible to rescue them?

NIKOLAI: If you talk to me once more I will come over there and kick you.

Silence.

No, it is not possible, Matty.

MATTY *has tears in his eyes.*

There's no need to cry as well, you horrible big baby.

NIKOLAI *puts the embryos in the grass.*

If you're going to cry, will you cry away from here.

NIKOLAI *fastens the incubator lid. He stands up. He picks up the incubator.*

I hate you, Matty.

NIKOLAI *goes.*

MATTY *is still, with tears in his eyes.*

A pause.

He begins to sob. He goes to his rucksack and puts it on. He jiggles up and down to get it more comfortable.

NIKOLAI *enters. He stops.*

MATTY *looks at him.*

Matty, I have decided I must return the Grey Crane eggs to the nest.

MATTY: May I help you?

NIKOLAI: No. Please move away.

MATTY *moves away from the nest.*

NIKOLAI *takes the incubator to the nest. He kneels.*

MATTY: I'm sorry, Nikolai.

NIKOLAI: I think you are a boy who will always be sorry. I am sorry, too.

NIKOLAI *takes the pot egg from the nest. He stands up.*

I have decided I cannot leave you on your own.

He goes to MATTY. *He puts the egg into the rucksack.*

You did not fasten this.

MATTY: Didn't I?

NIKOLAI: No. Our belongings might have fallen out.

NIKOLAI *fastens the rucksack. He goes back to the nest. He kneels.*

MATTY *goes to the nest.*

I do not want you near me.

MATTY *kneels.*

I think you will always disagree with other people, Matty.

MATTY: If I tell your father, Nikolai.

A slight pause.

NIKOLAI: I do not know what I must tell him.

MATTY: If I tell your father, will you tell my grandmother? She'll kill me.

NIKOLAI: Kill you? Like you killed the Siberian eggs? I do not think your grandmother will kill you, Matty.

A slight pause.

This was my father's big trust in me.

NIKOLAI *opens the incubator.*

Do you want her to kill me instead?

MATTY: No.

MATTY *stands up. He walks away from the nest.*

NIKOLAI *transfers the Grey Crane eggs. He closes the incubator.*

I wouldn't blame her if she did kill me.

A slight pause.

NIKOLAI: If I tell her it was partly my fault. She will not kill both of us.

NIKOLAI *stands up.*

We could say the Siberian eggs are the ones on the nest, Matty?

A slight pause.

MATTY: What about those? You've just transferred them.

NIKOLAI: I could put them back in the incubator? When we return it would seem the same.

A pause.

MATTY: No.

A slight pause.

Well, unless you want to?

NIKOLAI: My father would never forgive me if I lied to him.

NIKOLAI *offers his hand.*

If I shake your hand will you help me tell my father what has happened?

MATTY *slowly walks to* NIKOLAI.

NIKOLAI *picks up the incubator.*

MATTY: I'll tell him, Nikolai.

The two boys shake hands.